Presented To

_____

From

_____

Date

_____

My Heart, My Horse

My Heart, My Horse

Darlene Kemper

Drawbaugh Publishing Group
444 Allen Drive
Chambersburg, PA 17202

Paperback ISBN: 978-1-941746-15-8

eBook ISBN: 978-1-941746-16-5

For worldwide Distribution, Printed in the United States.

1 2 3 4 5 6 7 8 9 10 / 18 17 16 15

Table of Contents

Foreword

What follows is a collection of short stories about incidents in the life of Darlene Kemper. There are a few things about the writer that, while not apparent from the beginning, have much to do with these happenings. In some cases, the traits of this writer may have influenced some of these events, not only in the telling of the story, but also its outcome.

Darlene Kemper seemed, from the day I first met her as a college student, to face every aspect of her life with an unusual amount of zeal and fortitude. She came to me wanting to learn to ride, and she wanted to do it *well*. No detail of anything would be left unattended and nothing would be left to chance if there was some way that she could positively affect the outcome. In other words, Darlene has lived her life with as much passion as anyone I have ever known.

That is not to say that everything she did had to set a record of some kind. These stories are often written about the small incidents that make up everyday life. Her eye for detail and her storytelling capture the beauty in these small but important moments. These events, and the outcomes, were very important to her and thus to the people around her. She recognizes the contributions of the school horses as well as the show horses. She sees the value in working with those who have talent, and those whose work ethic exceeds their native abilities.

As I read this book, I learned many things about her life that I had never known. And at the same time, I could have added some stories of my own that involved her in my own life, things that were certainly memorable to me. Reading her book, I became keenly aware that we share some common threads in our philosophy of life. And, there are also things that she seemed to always know, and have, for some reason, taken me a lifetime to learn.

Horse people dedicate their lives to working around horses. It is very easy to become totally consumed in every horse, every horse show, and all of the details involved in the daily routine of breeding, teaching, and training. Quickly it can become a life where nothing else in the world seems as important as your work. I have spent a lot of years caught up in trying to do and be the best I could be at my job. But Darlene has always known better than to be caught up in that syndrome. Yes, she is a very hard worker and the results show the success of that hard work. But she and I both know that our children and any positive influence we can have on the lives of others is all that really matters in the end. She, with her passion for life, has done a beautiful job at both of these things.

As you read these stories, I hope you will keep this thought in the back of your mind. One of her contributions is that she has raised two children that are now touching and improving the lives of many others.

The oldest daughter, Diana, has adopted Darlene's world view of equality and loving, regardless of skin color, wealth or status. This daughter has adopted two children, one in the U. S., and another from Ethiopia, giving these children safety, love and, of course, the opportunity to ride and enjoy horses. Diana, a history teacher in the Rockingham County school system, and her husband, have added two "homegrown" children to her family. All of these children prowl around the farm and barn with Darlene's whole-hearted blessings.

The second daughter, Brooke, has become a horse professional, training and competing on the Grand Prix level and continuing in the horse life introduced to her by her mother. It is obvious that this daughter carries the family gene for equine appreciation and "attention to detail", and she has become an excellent rider and horsewoman.

– Sarah Coaching a Student

Darlene has made a marked difference in the lives she has touched, including mine.

Once I started reading this book, I could hardly put it down until I had read it all. Here's hoping you will feel the same way!

Sarah Irvine

Acknowledgements

My most humble and sincere thanks to:
All those who have contributed material for this book, both equine and human. It has been a pleasure and I could not have done this without you.

Joan Goode, my Mom, for your support and encouragement.

My children, Diana and Brooke, whose love and involvement with horses continues to give me great pleasure.

Whit, my husband, who tolerated crazy schedules and endless conversations.

John Sze, friend, confidant and creative genius behind Sze Designs and Graceful Manor Publications. Thanks for your advice, direction and support.

Sue, for believing in me and for being ever-ready for adventure.

Angela and Becka, who let me practice teaching and mothering, and survived.

Sarah, for putting my foot on the path.

God, who gave me the gifts which I gratefully acknowledge. I am ever-striving to use them well.

The horses I have known and loved. Show horse or school horse, you have all been Champions. You have been the motivation for the writing of this book. May you live on through these stories. I will never forget you.

Those who pick up this book, purchase it and read it. You are holding a piece of my heart.

– Mark and Darlene 1958

Chapter 1

In the Beginning...

"The wind of heaven is that which blows between a horse's ears."
Arabian Proverb

The old brown pickup truck came rumbling down the road, bouncing and chattering, announcing its arrival. Behind it was a rattletrap horse trailer, looking like a tin can on wheels. Inside, however, was the most beautiful thing I had ever seen! The small black Shetland pony inside was certainly not of noble origin, so shaggy that I couldn't tell if it was male or female. Young or old, that did not matter to me, nor did I have any knowledge of its life history or circumstances. All I remember is that when the old man unloaded this little creature, I was in love.

Being 5 years old, my youthful eyes saw the pony with all the wonder and fantasy such a moment could conjure. I didn't see her common head, or her rough, shaggy coat. I didn't notice her cheap tack or the manure on her feet. Such things are easily noticed now when I look at the picture commemorating the event. For one dollar, children could ride upon her little back in a tiny western saddle. For an extra dollar you could get a Polaroid picture of the event, which seemed to make the parents happy. The neighborhood kids would congregate on the edge of the road, waiting their turns. The ride probably lasted two minutes or less but it was enough,

enough to set in motion a love that would last me a lifetime. The die was cast, the deed was done and an unending love for horses was launched.

We lived in that east Baltimore neighborhood for another year, and every time the "pony man" would come to town, I was the first in line. Sometimes, if the line was not too long, my Mother would let me ride twice. This did not happen very often however, because my little brother, Mark, caught on to this event and he wanted a turn as well. The arrival of the pony into that neighborhood, which could be counted as just barely out of the city, made a great splash of an event for the children there, me included. There, amongst the sameness of the row houses and the miniscule yards surrounding them, a pony was like a gift from God. I wonder if any of the other children were bitten by the bug that causes horse fever. Who knows? When we moved away in 1960, I mourned the fact that I would likely never seen the "pony man" again. I was too young to know that other locations might have similar opportunities. My heart was broken.

Lucky for me, the pony-withdrawal would not last too long. We moved to suburbia! Edgewood Meadows was a new community, just being developed on the site of a large farm. An elderly man, Mr. Hansen, sold his property to a developer and he continued to live just down the road from our new house. Being the ripe old age of seven now, I began to explore the neighborhood, which didn't take long as we were only the fourth house in the developing community. There were lots of hills and very few roads just yet, so my parents felt perfectly comfortable with me playing outside unsupervised for long periods of time. It was nothing for me to go on a trek after breakfast and wander about for several hours. After all, we had moved to the country!

On one of my jaunts, I discovered that where the road stopped, a large meadow started. In the meadow were several large draft horses. Kind of orange with white manes and tales, I am certain now that they were of Belgian origin, probably left over from the working days of the large farm. Sleeping in the sun, they stood perfectly still as I climbed up the four-board fence. Perched atop the rail, I feasted my eyes on their beauty. They were roly-poly round, up to their hocks in new grass and shining in the morning sun. I stayed for a long time, dreaming about how it would feel to sit upon those ample backs, breathing in the smell of horse. To this day, I welcome the smell of horse. How can I describe it? Horses have their own smell, sweet, earthy and often tinged with moisture, sweat or rain. Those who have appreciated this aroma will recognize the description. Closing my eyes, I could hear the bees buzzing, feel the breeze lift and ruffle my hair. I could hear the breathing of the mares, the occasional stomp as they warned the flies away. (I had decided that they were indeed mares, since I didn't notice any boy parts.) Discovering these horses was like a grandsecret, and this became my special place that I would visit every day that summer.

Day after day I visited, and the horses became very comfortable with my presence. Often, they would take their naps close to the fence, where I had become bold enough to reach over and pet their massive shoulders. Pulling up handfuls of grass, I offered this snack to them. As they were already standing in knee-deep pasture, it is a wonder they took any notice of this offering, but most of the time they would obligingly sniff and mouth the handfuls I offered, never once biting the tips of my fingers off. I knew nothing about feeding a horse from the flat of my hand. I still have ten fingers, which speaks favorably about the gentle nature of these giant mares.

About a month or so into my visits, I began to grow restless. What would it feel like to sit upon their backs? How could I get up so high? They wore no halters, so there was no way to lead or steer. One day, as they stood sleeping next to the fence, I climbed up to the top rail. Reaching out, I ruffled the ample mane of the closest mare, fingering those flaxen strands. The mare was unconcerned as I played with her mane. I visualized climbing onto her back. It would be so easy! I was so close. And the mares were very comfortable with me, so…Standing on the top rail I grabbed mane and plopped myself onto her back. This, of course, was an unexpected turn of events for the mare, and she startled awake. I felt her spine stiffen under my seat, and grabbed a tighter hold of the white mane. Off we went at a trot. I was scared out of my mind, but also deliriously happy. I was riding! I was Alec riding the Black Stallion. I was Elizabeth Taylor in National Velvet! The wind was in my hair and tears were in my eyes. My world had become unlimited. No matter that this was an old draft mare motivated into a lumbering trot. In my mind we were flying!

Down through the field she trotted. At first I was coping well, but as the downhill grade became more pronounced and the mare's trot became faster, I began to flop up and down on her back. Perhaps it was this that caused her to suddenly take alarm, or perhaps she just wanted to go for little romp through the field. Either way, as the mare picked up speed, my precarious perch became less secure with every step. I clutched her mane in my hands and leaned low into her neck, clinging on like a tiny monkey. The thrill of the ride was in my soul, still overriding the danger messages from my brain. I could not exactly visualize how this ride would end, but it occurred to me that I was not in control. I didn't care! Tears streamed from my eyes as we galloped down through the meadow. It was everything I had ever dreamed of, and more! Almost a spiritual experience for this 7 year old, I soaked up every nuance of the ride: the mare's powerful quarters pushing us along, her shoulder moving under my hands, her mane streaming out beyond my body, whipping my eyes. The smell of her, sweet and sweaty, far overpowered any feelings of fear that I should have had. It is not that I was extraordinarily brave, it was that I was extraordinarily in love. No matter how it ended, the ride was worth it.

The thrill of the ride was in my soul

All of a sudden, the end of the field and the fence line came into view. The mare swung sharply left. Now, I had just barely been able to stay on as we traveled in a straight line. There was nothing to prepare me for a hard left, and my body swung out to the right. Luckily, she kept going left, and her feet never came close to me as we parted company. As I fell, it seemed as though time changed to slow motion. I remember sailing through the air. I felt warm and almost weightless, like a leaf. I remember the feeling and the suspense. And then came the fall. Unceremoniously, I landed hard, no longer cushioned by those lovely large muscles, or that warm country air. I landed hard, knocking the breath out of me. It was really the first pain that I remember in life, and for a moment I was stunned and scared. On the ground, I gasped for breath, although my lungs seemed reluctant to work. Then a thought hit me, and scared the pain away. "What if someone saw me? What if they think I'm hurt and tell my parents? What if I never get to visit the mares again?" These thoughts hurt worse than the sudden landing on the ground.

Quickly I scampered to my feet, anxiously scanning the field around me, hoping against hope that no one had witnessed my ride, and especially not my fall. Luckily, I saw no one. Gingerly I tried to walk, my chest still aching with the effort to breathe. God must protect children. Maybe there really are guardian angels, I don't know, but someone was watching out for me that day. Thankfully, however, the watching was not by earthly eyes!

As I slowly walked back up the hill toward the fence line, I heard a quiet rustling in the grass behind me. It was her, the big mare, and she followed me back up the hill. "I'll just bet that she is sad that I fell off" I thought, in true young child ego-centric fashion, followed by "I wonder if she had as much fun as I did?" Getting to the fence, I painfully climbed up one side and down the other, vowing to come back the next day and try again.

It was actually several days until I was able to return, as my little body was rather shook up and battered. I couldn't tell my parents where the bruises came from, so I blamed them on a bicycle fall. Being somewhat reckless with my bike, this little lie was pretty believable and no further questions were asked. Instinctively, I knew that if I confessed that I got hurt jumping onto the back of a very large horse, without the advantage of saddle or bridle…well I knew that my horse visits would come to an abrupt end. Bicycles were something my parents understood; love of horses was unknown to them, as they had grown up largely in the city. I decided that it was better that I should protect them from the truth, sparing them worry… and giving me more opportunities to try that ride again.

So, that's how the horse bug bit me. No amount of antidote can cure such a case. And, for that matter, I never want to be cured. To stop loving equines would be to deny a part of my soul.

CB&O

From ancient times, before recorded history, the horse has played a part in the development of human civilization. From cave drawings dating back to the Stone Age, we know that prehistoric man probably hunted the horse for meat. (I forgive prehistoric man for this grave error, as they had other things to occupy their time, like inventing the wheel and such.) It is difficult to pinpoint the exact time when man began to domesticate the horse, but many sources cite evidence that horses were bred and kept in captivity around 2500 B. C. Evidence such as "bit" wear on the teeth of excavated skeletons, and soil changes in certain areas indicating equine containment and lots of equine manure, show us a pattern of equine evolution from food source to beast of burden. Horses assisted humankind by plowing their fields, pulling their wagons, carrying their soldiers into battle, helping to scout out new peoples to conquer and new areas to settle. Horses pulled both chariots and plows, helped to wage war, defend settlements, provided mounted games and companionship. Before long, horse ownership became a symbol of elevated status in societies. Brides were purchased with horses as the bride price. Horses were buried with rulers, to ensure that their masters would have swift horses in their next lives. In some nomadic cultures, a too-small tent meant the wife slept outside while the warrior's horse slept in, because a swift and brave horse made the difference between life and death.

Equine evolution from food source to beast of burden

Horses were important wherever they were found. From the Greeks to the Arabian cultures, in nomadic cultures or city-dwelling peoples, horses contributed heavily to the development of new lands, trading routes and mobile armies. Horses traveled to the New World with the Spaniards. They helped to conquer the Russian Steppes. They carried settlers into the American West. The American cattle herder became known as a cowboy, and treasured a good saddle horse as much as any. Once again, the difference between living and dying came down to the reliability of that cowboy's horse.

By the time of World War II, the horse was no longer relied upon as a means of transportation. Trucks and tanks replaced horse-power. While there are still areas of the world where nomadic people live symbiotically with their horses, and while cowboys still ride the range with their cowponies, the horse has largely become a creature of companionship and sport. Thus, the horse has come to transcend the boundaries of its utilitarian past.

So, somehow and someway, the bond between humans and equines has continued to be strong. I like to think that equine DNA and human DNA are intertwined, if not genetically then at least developmentally and spiritually.

When you examine the nature of the horse, you see clearly the influence his "prey" status has on his personality. Horses hate loud noises, startle at things that come at them from behind, where they are most vulnerable because of the blind spot in their vision. When frightened, horses would rather run away than stand and fight, because they know by instinct that they are not good fighters. Horses are "herd" animals, finding safety and security in numbers.

Humans are "predators". We are meat eaters who use tools to kill things. We "think" our way out of trouble, and are often happier to confront rather than console. We are "take charge" beings, by and large, and tend to want to subjugate others to our will. That is not all bad, when it comes to the horse-human relationship. Horses, in a wild herd, look to the dominant horse for direction. Horses naturally form a pecking order. And so, they are usually quite happy to have their riders become their leaders. They offer us their speed, agility, versatility and companionship in exchange for our protection, the providing of their food and shelter, and our companionship, as well.

Of late, we have begun to take the advice of ancient horsemen such as Xenophon, a Greek historian and essayist, who wrote long treatises on "The Art of Horsemanship" in the fourth or fifth century B. C. He advocated the horse be treated with kindness rather than force. He wrote extensively of the careful and thoughtful training of the horse. In "The Art of Horsemanship" he wrote:

> *For what a horse does under constraint...he does without under-standing, and with no more grace than a dancer would show if he were whipped and goaded. Under such treatment, horse and man alike will do much more that is ugly than graceful.*

Xenophon's thoughts on horsemanship have inspired countless horse fanciers, including modern horsemen and women. The modern phrase "horse whisperer" applies to a style of horsemanship that involves reading the physical cues of the horse to find the correct time to introduce training. Natural horsemanship involves observing equines in their natural herd behaviors, and utilizing this information to communicate effectively with the horse. Current thought is that training without fear accomplishes much more than achieving the subjugation of the horse through brutality. I am grateful for this development in horse-training philosophy. I believe that fear is the mind killer, and neither horses nor humans can learn well when fearful.

– Darlene and Mark 2011

We can document the continuing relationship between equines and humans, and see the position of the horse in human lives as it moved from food source to companion. Recognizing our continuing fascination with the horse, I do think that this bond is in some way in-born.

So, if you plop out of the womb with the horse-fascination gene, there is no cure for you. It is best to just relax and go with it.

– Darlene on Campus

Chapter 2

Adventures with Sarah

"Great riders are not great solely by virtue of their talents. They are great because of their passion."

Anonymous

On a sunny morning in 1973, I set off to find a barn and a riding instructor. I left my apartment in Harrisonburg, and had high hopes for finding the "woman who teaches riding" in Pleasant Valley, a small town nearby. Having loved horses all my life, I felt determined to DO something about that pull I felt in my gut every time I saw an equine of any type. A friend had told me about this barn, and so…the hunt began.

Turning off the main road onto dirt and gravel, I felt like I was indeed heading into a more rural setting. It was the spring, and birds were calling, wild flowers along the roadside were blooming and I felt hopeful…hopeful for the warm weather, hopeful for a new adventure, hopeful for a new chapter in my life. You might say I had no idea how important this chapter would become.

Driving along, I came to a farm on the right side of the road. Many barns, all looking about half finished, were scattered on the road side of the property. Horses were *everywhere!* Large and small, bay, chestnut, grey, they dotted the landscape. I had *arrived!*

Pulling up to a blue travel trailer parked at the top of the hill, I parked and got out to seek the proprietor of this establishment.

I was nearly trembling with excitement, breathing in all the farm smells. You know you are a born horse lover when even the smell of horses and manure makes you smile. I did not see anyone out and about, so I was wondering if I should knock on the door of the trailer. It was about 9: 30 a. m., and I didn't want to wake anybody. Country people get up with the chickens, don't they? And there were chickens in abundance here, pecking the ground and acting as the clean-up committee for little bits of corn found in the manure deposits here and there. That might sound a little disgusting to some, picking out your breakfast from piles of poop, but chickens find this to be recycling at its finest.

The hands that rested on the railing of the porch were working hands

While I was preoccupied with the scenery and trying to make my decision about knocking on the door, I had failed to notice that someone had emerged from the blue trailer.

"Can I help you?" asked the woman on the porch. The voice was rather flat, as though I was intruding. Although I noticed the slightly irritated inflection, I was resolved to press on. Turning to the woman, I saw that she was still wearing a housecoat of blue and white stripes, somewhat worn and looking rumpled from sleep. Her hair, a cornhusk blond, was pulled back in a loose pony tail. She looked to be a no-nonsense kind of person, a cut-to-the-chase and get on with it sort. She was definitely my idea of "country", so why was she still in sleep clothes? I would learn later in time that she had just had some type of surgery the day before, and so was in recuperation mode.

"Oh, ah, well, I was…I wanted…I am looking for the woman who teaches horseback riding here," I managed to stammer out. Not usually at a loss for words, I was so excited I could hardly express myself.

The blond woman just looked at me, and for a long minute, she said not a word. "She's checking me out!" I thought. "She's *really* checking me out and deciding if I am worthy of her time." Now a quick inventory of my outfit would not exactly scream "equestrian". My tennis shoes were virgin-white, my jeans were NOT wranglers, and my t-shirt and sweater were more college-crowd than barn rat.

Thoughts screaming in my head and eager not to be dismissed lightly, I quickly offered aloud, "I'm really serious about this! I want to learn."

She turned her face into the sun, eyes closed. In that minute, I was in love! She was the ultimate *earth woman*, sleepy-eyed, no make-up (who cares) and vaguely aggravated by my unscheduled presence. She exuded strength, quiet strength and a calmness that captured me. The hands that rested on the railing of the porch were working hands, short nails, some broken off from use, but strong and capable hands. Her pony tail was pulled back unceremoniously, strictly for getting her hair out of the way. There was no pretention of curls or style.

I guess I should mention at this point that I was not drawn in a sexual way. Fact is, I like men just fine, in fact maybe a little too well in certain stages of my life. This was not a romantic attraction in the traditional sense of the word, but more a kind of epiphany experience that I still remember clearly to this day. This was a woman I wanted to get to know, and add to that, *she was a horse woman!*

Turning back to me, she said, "Come back on Tuesday at 2. I'm not teaching today." It was a statement, not a question. There was no, "if that is convenient." Clearly her no nonsense comment was meant to convey that if I was serious I would be there. If 2 p. m. on Tuesday did not suit me, then so be it.

"I'll be here," came from my lips just as she made a slight wave of her hand and turned back to her door. That was it. It was a start.

Tuesday, at 2 p.m. came. I had actually arrived at 1:45, guessing the blond woman would not take tardiness well. In fact, she did comment on my arrival. "Well, I see that you showed up. Kim will teach you today."

"Oh no," I thought. "She's passing me off to an underling. She doesn't think I am serious!" You would have thought I was being refused membership to some prestigious club, such was my temporary heartache. Being basically a Pollyanna, I decided to make the most of my lesson, even if it wasn't with the *earth woman*. As it turns out, Kim was a perfectly good, competent instructor. She mounted me on a plain bay school horse (it felt like I was riding the grand champion hunter of all time), and began teaching the basic skills needed to navigate an equine.

"When you need to stop, pull back with both hands toward your middle, and say whoa." "No pull, not *yank!* That's her mouth you are grabbing when you yank the reins." Kim was patient and repeated things so she could be understood, even by a newbie like me. In that first lesson, I got the basics of walk, trot and canter. I was green enough not to realize that very few people, with as little actual experience as I had, actually get to canter on their first ride. I did not realize that Kim was pleased with my progress. All that I knew was that I had to have more!

I began to eat less and ride more

On one of my early Kim lessons, she took me out into the field, beyond the riding ring. As we walked and trotted through the fields, I was in my own little world. The trees and the grass were greening up with the increasing temperatures. Legs wrapped around the barrel of my horse of the day, I could smell the mixed aromas of horse sweat and leather, and I felt there was nothing better. *But I was wrong!*

"Canter!" Kim ordered. "In the field?" I thought. "No ring rail, out in the open?" We both began to canter across the field, tears squeezing from my eyes, my heart in my mouth. The horse was a saint, staying steady and quiet. I could do no more than cling on and let the horse do her job. Her name was Molly, and she took care of me for this first field canter. Now this *was* a little taste of heaven.

Being a poor college sophomore, I had very little money. My parents would send me a food allowance each month, and that was about it. So, you guessed it, I began to eat less and ride more, finding ways to stretch the food dollars, (can you say Ramen noodles?), so that I could use the bulk of my money for lessons. My parents, basically city-raised, did not understand my horse fascination, and so riding lessons had never been a part of my childhood. Now, being away at college, I was determined to ride, and I saw no need to alarm them. What they didn't know wouldn't cause them anxiety or hurt them. I just had to do it.

After five lessons or so, Kim informed me that Sarah, the blond woman, would take over teaching me. What and why didn't matter really, because I was glad just to be there. But I guess I was moving up. All through the spring of 1973, I rode first once per week, then twice and finally up to three times per week. Every lesson brought more challenges.

"Don't just sit there, "Sarah explained. "Control your body, keep your eyes forward, your heels down for balance." One day she said, "I like your hands. You don't use them for balance and you don't pull on the horse's mouth." (Thank you, Kim!)

She likes my hands! I almost fainted. Sarah was then, and continues to this day to be, sparing with compliments. If you get one, you'd better treasure it. And I did.

CR8O

As my barn experiences continued, I learned that the farm was owned and operated by an African American man named Charles. Now, this being the 1970's in southern United States, this should have seemed strange to me. One just didn't see that many black people in business-ownership positions and especially not in the horse world. Evidently, Charles had been employed as a barn manager at another barn in the city of Harrisonburg, and Sarah had been his main rider there. When a barn fire shut that business down, Charles was out of work and so had decided to open up his own farm in this location. He named it Poverty Hill, probably because of the number of pennies left in his pocket each month after the expenses were paid.

However, I really didn't register that Charles was in anyway unusual, having his own farm and a blond exercise jockey named Sarah in southern Virginia in the 1970s. I think my own Mother deserves credit for that.

As I was growing up in the 1950s on the outskirts of Baltimore, life was probably not easy for people of color. There were separate bathrooms, problems with seating on buses, segregated schools (officially or unofficially). Your station in life was largely determined by the color of your skin. But not at my Mother's house! Yes, we did have a cleaning lady who helped my young Mother with the laundry and cleaning and care of her growing family. Her name was Lucille, and we all loved her. On the days that Lucille came, she would go about her various duties, vacuuming, washing clothes, and so on. Mom had her chores and we children spent the morning playing. At noon, everyone stopped their various and sundry activities and converged at the dining table, where one and all had a lunch prepared by my Mom. Lucille dined with us at the request of my Mother. At first hesitant, she soon loosened up a bit and we had fairly lively conversation during the lunch break.

But today, my Mom became a GIANT, at least in my eyes!

Somehow, whether through the window or by word of mouth, somehow the neighbors got wind of this routine. They thought it rather unseemly that a "nigger" (their word, not mine) was allowed to eat with the white folks. Now I had not actually heard the "n" word until the day that "Mrs. Ivy", a neighbor, knocked on our front door. My Mom and several of her children, including me, went to the door. Opening it, we saw the "posse"! Behind Mrs. Ivy stood five other neighborhood ladies, all with stern looks on their faces. She cut right to the chase.

"We don't allow niggers to eat at our tables, and you shouldn't either!" She pronounced. It isn't proper and it has to stop. Now!" She had an explosive look on her face and even I, at age 5, could tell that she took great strength from the women standing behind her, as she kept looking back at them for confirmation.

Now, my Mom was never a large woman. In her prime she stood about 5 foot 2 inches. And she was NEVER an outspoken woman, keeping her own council and always playing the peacemaker in our family. But today, my Mom became a GIANT, at least in my eyes! Drawing herself up to her tallest posture, she looked Mrs. Ivy straight in the eyes and said, "My lunch guests are none of your business. Now, I will thank you ladies to get off of MY porch. And I WILL continue to have lunch with whomever I choose. Good bye!"

Mom slammed the door closed, and then huffed back to the table, followed by her brood of youngsters. Lucille, who had to overhear at least some of this exchange, started to jump up. "Lucille," my Mom said calmly (although I noticed her face was red)," please sit down and finish eating your lunch with us."

Nothing more was said about this event inside the walls of our house. The neighborhood was all abuzz about it for a while, and people looked at us funny, but I really didn't care. Don't think Mom did either. But a powerful message came to me and my siblings that day. The color of a person's skin was a minor thing. More important was the color of his or her heart, and the integrity of their work and their word. Mom gave us a lesson that I have never forgotten. I doubt that Mrs. Ivy ever wavered in her self-righteous bigotry, but Mom gave her children an example to live by and I am ever grateful for that.

And so, seeing Charles as the owner of the barn that catered largely to white riders never really seemed odd to me. I was more interested in his horse knowledge and his expertise. He treated me kindly and gave me opportunities to ride his horses, and I learned a great deal from him as well as from Sarah. My friendship with him continued until his death in 2012.

ᘓᘔᑐ

Being associated with this barn and becoming more and more involved in the horse culture (and yes, horse people are a unique, adventurous, opinionated and fun group of folks), I began to ride as often as possible. Still in college, I really had little money, and so had to find creative ways to pay for my horse activities.

Sarah, within a year after I had met her, married and had a child, a very cute little girl. And with babies comes the need for diapers!!! "O. K., I thought, "here is a service that I can render to Sarah, in exchange for riding lessons for me!" And so, I became her diaper service! For the next two years, we bartered diapers for lessons, giving me time to graduate from school and get a job. Although some might think washing stinky baby diapers was a nasty trade, I was thrilled with it. I had a great washer and dryer in my apartment, and I had a burning desire to learn everything I could about horses. This was definitely a win-win situation!

Soon, I was attending horse shows, going fox hunting, attending clinics, exercising other people's horses, anything that would aid in my crash course in equine appreciation. And there *were* a few crashes along the way! Regarding a certain amount of falls as part of the process, I was rarely seriously injured. Broke my tailbone once or twice, hit my head a few times (let's hear it for good riding helmets, which I wore), broke my nose (it's so easy to do when the brims of hard hats those days were very hard), etc. One very serious injury occurred a few years later, but that is, of course, another story.

> *"Remember, there is a difference between bravery and stupidity."*

Recalling my first foxhunting experience brings me fond memories. On a crisp autumn day, Sarah hauled two horses to the Rockbridge Hunt grounds. Because she had only a two horse trailer at that time, she had chosen to bring a horse for me and one for another student, Henry. Excited though I was, I was hesitant to go off on a new adventure without her, both because I hated to leave her behind while we took her horses to hunt, and because she was the one who had fox hunted before. Experience is a good thing, and can sometimes avert disaster. Sarah insisted, however, and so Henry and I mounted up. He was riding his own horse, and I was riding a horse that Sarah provided for me, a four year old half-thoroughbred.

Leaning close to me, Sarah looked me in the eyes and said, "Now this colt has never foxhunted, but he is kind and reasonably quiet. So, give him a good ride, and he will be just fine. Jump what seems possible. Leave the biggest coops alone." I felt a twinge of anxiety about the "never hunted" part, but my excitement and adrenaline won over. I was going foxhunting!

Just before we departed, Sarah called me to her side once again. This time she gave me a piece of advice that I will never forget. "Remember, there is a difference between bravery and stupidity."

While I was yet pondering the meaning of those words, the hunt began. "Oh yeah, this is **very** good advice," I thought, and I used it that day and on many other occasions throughout my life.

The hunting was lovely that day…hacking through the wooded areas and meadows to the location where the Hunt Master cast the hounds. Sounding his horn, he encouraged the hounds to get to work, and soon we were running through fields, dodging trees in the trappy country, all bound in pursuit of the wily fox. I am always glad that the fox knows where his den is, and so has the advantage over the hounds, who simply follow his sent. I loved watching the hounds work, noses to the ground, sniffing out their quarry with a fierce determination. There is something magical about watching hounds work, and that magic is enhanced when they begin to cry and then take off on the chase. Then all the foxhunting field takes off after the hounds. We galloped that day for what seemed hours. Reality is altered when the wind whips tears from your eyes, and you are entirely caught up in the hunt. Your job is to keep up, jumping over jumps, negotiating water crossings, scampering up hillsides more suited to goats than horses. In the end, you achieve a great deal of satisfaction, having dealt with the obstacles that Mother Nature has provided, and having *survived*.

Upon our return to the trailer-parking area, Sarah was eager to hear about our day. I think, secretly, she was pleased to see us—no injuries and jubilant! Henry and I regaled her with stories of the beauty and excitement of the hunt, our near-brushes with disaster and our brilliant riding. (Remember, horse people can spin tales just as big or bigger than fishermen. Thought you'd want to know!)

Another adventure with Sarah occurred a few years after the first hunt. By now I had my own horse, a quirky half thoroughbred/ half appaloosa named Buddy. Buddy could be a decent show horse at times, being athletic and also being a very good mover. But he left a lot to be desired in the field. Still, he is what I had. So, when Sarah invited me to do the Middleburg Hunt Point to Point with her, I expressed some concern.

"I've never done a Point to Point and Buddy is certainly not a race horse!" I laughed.

"Oh, just come for the fun of it," Sarah said; "You can just hunt along, going at your own pace."

For the uninitiated, a Point to Point is a race, cross-country over jumps. In the founding days of this style of racing, participants literally raced from point to point, the "points" being the steeples of churches in the area. The race could be a distance of seven miles or so, sometimes more. This race was seven miles, and the rider encounters the obstacles native to the Hunt sponsoring the race. In the case of Middleburg, the race traversed fields, wooded areas, a wide creek crossing, wood panel jumps, stone jumps, and so on. It is an exciting ride, to say the least.

Sarah rode a thoroughbred horse she was legging-up (the process of getting the horse fit) for the timber races, also sponsored by various Hunt Clubs in Virginia. Her horse was lean and mean, ready to run and jump, a little difficult to control. I was riding my Buddy, ill-suited for this job, but game enough. Sally A., another of Sarah's riders, would also accompany us, riding "Debbie", a young thoroughbred mare.

Tacked up and ready(?), the three of us joined the rest of the riders for this race at the starting line. I knew I was in trouble when they stretched the white starting line across the field, and raised the starting **pistol!** (As an aside, I might mention that Peter Winants, then editor of The *Chronicle of the Horse*, was also riding in this race. Middleburg folk are *into* this event!) The horses became agitated, sensing that something was about to go down. And down it came! The pistol sounded, the starting line dropped, and twenty-two horses leaped into action!

Now, to say that I was ill-prepared for this event would be an understatement. I had intended to just "hunt along" on this ride, never intending to be competitive or speedy, just along for the experience. I did not account for the competitive drive that horses have! The bit in my horse's mount was a rubber snaffle, for crying out loud, one used in the show ring, and one that is of very little use when twenty-two horses burst forward at the start of the race. Buddy was bound and determined to keep up, and there was little I could do to discourage him. I found myself solidly in the middle of the pack when we reached the first narrow passage. We had started in a wide field, which quickly emptied into a path that ran along a creek on the right and a large bank of rock and dirt on the left. The path was very narrow, allowing room for one horse only. To the right, the path was lined by barbed wire fencing, designed to keep cattle from going down to the water.

Into this slim path we charged, all twenty-two riders trying to get there ahead of the one next to them. In my case, the rider behind me decided to pass me! Barging in on my left (the bank side), he proceeded to try to squeeze me toward the barbed wire and the creek.

"Oh, no you don't!" I thought. "You are not pushing me toward the barbed wire, and you are not getting ahead of me!" Ok, so I guess at this point I had caught the race fever, too. When I refused to yield, I got a taste of what horse competition can become. This rider, personally unknown to me, took his bat (a leather covered stick used to encourage a horse to go forward faster), and began to smack MY horse with it! This was some kind of equine road rage. Now I saw red. Clearly this was not fair, and would have been penalized by the stewards (officials), but there were no stewards at this spot. I had to drop back or risk being forced into the barbed wire and over the bank.

When the narrow path opened once again into a field, I urged my horse forward, determined now to catch the rider ahead of me. Catch him I did, as my horse was faster (who knew?) and just about as pissed off as I was. Heading toward a large hedge crossing (a jump made out of hedge greenery—some kind of bushes), I urged my horse forward. As we neared the hedge, the other rider's horse was now galloping at my horse's hip, a half-horse distance farther away from the jump than I was. And, predictably, when my horse jumped *over* the jump, his horse left the ground at the same time. Being too far away at the take-off, his horse jumped onto and into the hedge, where the rider fell off, landing in the bushes. All I could think was, "Couldn't have happened to a *nicer* guy!"

By the way, at such race meets, there are outriders, members of the sponsoring hunt, who help with any difficulties that may result from the day's activities. The catch loose horses, assist fallen riders, keep folks on course, etc. In this case, they came to the aid of the fallen rider and his horse.

On we went. By now, Buddy had settled into a strong rhythmic gallop. I loved the feel of his power and energy below me. For just a few moments, I was lulled into this amazing euphoria, a feeling of power and strength and oneness with the horse. I felt that I could do anything! Perhaps this is the feeling, this unity of horse and human, that has bonded equines and humans down through the ages.

Running along, we entered a wooded area. At this location, I encountered Sarah. Her horse, very fit and being built more for speed in the flatlands that maneuverability in the woods, had blasted into the trees. Unfortunately, she had been unable to rate his speed, and he ran her leg into a tree. She knew immediately that it was broken, and had somehow gotten the horse to pull up. She couldn't continue the race with such an injury, so the outriders were helping her. I tried to pull up (stop) . Sarah waived me on. "Keep going," she instructed, "there's nothing you can do for me right now. I'll see you at the end. Finish the race."

The race continued! Jump after jump and mile after mile, Buddy and I galloped along. I noticed that recent rains had left large puddles of water pooled up on our path. Horses who are fit and moving quickly will often jump such unintended obstacles. Even though these puddles were not huge, the horses regarded them as suspicious and rather than splash through, they sometimes jumped! Sally, one of our group, had encountered just such a situation, and her horse *launched* itself over a big puddle on the ground, then landed badly and slipped. As horse and rider fell to the ground, Sally was unseated, and as the horse scrambled to get up, she stepped on Sally's back! It was at this point that I arrived on the scene.

Urgency was clear, but the words were not

Seeing Sally on the ground, I again tried to pull up to help her. The outriders were already there, one catching the horse and the other dismounted to help Sally. Sally yelled, "Go on. I've got help here."

The next hazard was water. Earlier, before the race began, I had noticed the riders for this race were dressed very well, wearing their best hunt coats, stock ties (a type of neck ware specific to this sport) and so on. From the waist down, however, their attire was not so good. Their boots and breeches looked worn and plain, clearly not matching their upper body clothing. I was about to find out why.

As I continued, I came to a place where the race participants needed to cross a stream, now swollen by the recent rains. The outrider on the far bank was yelling something to me as I approached. I couldn't make out the words, as the sounds of the hoof beats—mine and the other riders' horses—drowned out the words. "Watch out for the _____! Watch out _____!" Urgency was clear, but the words were not. As my horse leapt from the bank into the water, I suddenly discovered the missing words. "Watch out **for the HOLE!**" My horse pitched forward, grabbing for purchase on the creek bed below, but THERE WAS NONE! We were swimming! Water splashed up to my waist and poured into my custom riding boots. Uggg. Now I know why the dress code here had called for more casual lower-body clothes. No one wants to mess up $1,200 boots in the water!

Boots at this point were beyond consideration now, being full of creek water. I decided to just be glad that my horse could swim. In short order, we clamored up the bank on the other side.

I am certain that this is a *serious* race, a take-no-prisoner's kind of ride. Galloping along, we come to the next type of jump, stone walls build into the fence line. Anyone who has traveled through Middleburg, Virginia, has noticed the handsome stone walls lining some of the fields there. Built back in the 1800's, these rock walls are stately, beautiful and HARD! It is imperative to jump over these cleanly, as they do not fall down. The horse would fall before the stone wall jumps do. At this point, my horse had begun to tire. What had begun as powerful galloping strides, effortless and forward, now became more labored. Approaching the stonewalls, I used my own bat, tapping my horse's flank smartly, urging him forward. *I did not want to be the rider who falls off on the stones!*

Gamely, he cleared first one and then the other, crossing over a dirt road in between. The term for two jumps of this nature, close together, is an *in-and-out,* into the road with one jump and *out* of the road with the other. At this point, we were nearing the finish line. Seven miles of open country had been covered, with every kind of terrain possible.

Of our group of three, I was the only one still in the race, a quirk of fate to be sure. And of the twenty-two horses who had started the race, only 12 finished.

I learned several things that day:

1. When you go "just for the experience", the experience may be quite different than what you expect.
2. A "fit" race horse is a formidable force, and a jockey determined to win a race can show "road rage" like none other.
3. When legs meet trees, trees win! Sarah healed from this mishap eventually, and actually drove the horse van home that day…and then got her leg put in the cast. Quite a show of determination, but that leg has troubled her off and on for years.
4. Race horses don't like puddles…or shadows…or any other unexpected element in their path. And I sure didn't like leaving my friends, hurt and down, to finish a race.
5. And, perhaps most importantly, I learned to think on the fly, surviving a race for which neither my horse nor myself were prepared. And I got to experience "the feeling", the sheer joy of galloping flat out, wide open and running free…*and surviving.*

There are so many other stories I could add here, like the time Sarah made me hitch-hike to go get help for our horse van. The fuel had gelled due to the temperature being less than 20 degrees. So, coming down Interstate 81, our van had stalled and we seriously needed help. I didn't want to hitch-hike for help, getting picked up by a stranger. I still don't recommend it, but this man did take me to a gas station where I was able to get help for Sarah, the van and the horses. Lesson One: do what you have to do for the welfare of the horses. Lesson Two: Hitch-hiking is dangerous and scary. You may not get a nice person with your best interests at heart. I just got lucky. We have cellphones now. Use them! Lesson Three: In case of emergency, think "pepper spray"!

During this same period of time, I was working 9-5 at a law firm in Harrisonburg. Therefore, the only time I had for lessons was 6 a. m., even in the dead of winter. There were many mornings when I just wanted to curl up and stay in bed. But I was sure Sarah would be disappointed in me if I didn't make the effort to stay in training. Years later I would find out that she literally prayed that Henry, another early morning student, and I would not show up. But show up we did, day after day, surviving bitter cold, sharing Henry's all-too-well-used handkerchief for our runny noses.

Over the years, my relationship with Sarah deepened. What had begun as instructor and student became much more. Prior to our meeting, I had intended to follow a legal career, intending to be an attorney. However, Sarah was instrumental in setting my foot on another path. Through her mentorship, I became student, rider, horsewoman, and then a professional horsewoman in my own right. Sarah nurtured and strengthened my resolve to make horses my life and career. She taught me riding skills, and teaching skills. I gave riding lessons to some of her students for a year or two, before opening my own business.

She has watched me mature, develop my own business, build a farm and raise a family. Over the years, I have brought my daughters, both riders, to take occasional lessons with her. We have served together on the Board of Directors of the Southwest Virginia Hunter Jumper Association. We have each taken our turns being President of that Association. We have worked, shown, and ridden together. We have downed a few beers and drank a few bottles of wine while laughing or commiserating, as needed.

To me, every day is an adventure and *horse people* as a group are interesting, colorful, determined, eccentric, and especially prone to adventurous activities. *Sarah is surely one of these.*

Chapter 3

Dating is <u>Not</u> for the Faint Hearted

"Ride the horse in the direction it is going."
Werner Erhard

Things happen a little differently in the country, in lots of ways. I got an early introduction to that fact while I was dating Whit, who would one day become my husband. There are always farm chores to do, and somehow along the way we try to get in a little quality time together. I understood that, as I had a little farm of my own, with my horse keeping chores always looming large in my life.

One Friday night, prime dating time, Whit called me to say that he needed to cancel our date for that night. I was a little taken aback, and he must have heard that in my voice, so he added, "Unless you want to come along while I haul a pig for some friends." Turns out that he had forgotten a promise to pick up a butchering pig from the house of Tom and Sue Sipes, and haul it to the butcher, who would process it for their freezer. Whit's job was to load this pig onto his large farm truck, which had racks in the back for containment. This sounded interesting to me, and relatively easy, so I agreed to tag along. After all, a date is still a date, right?

So I changed my "going out to dinner clothes", and donned jeans, a sweater and boots, which seemed more appropriate for this outing. I did pick a nice sweater, in hues of purple and blue, and a pair of my better jeans (translation: no holes) . I smelled pretty good, being freshly showered and with a little dab of cologne. It was, after all, still a chance to spend some time with a handsome farmer. Shortly thereafter, Whit picked me up in an old Ford farm truck, complete with racks on the back. We bounced down the road to high adventure!

The "pig" was a "gilt" (a girl hog), weighing about 400 pounds

---

Arriving at the barn where the pig was housed, I got my first surprise. The "pig" was a "gilt" (a girl hog), weighing about 400 pounds or so! She was about the size of a small pony! At that time I knew nothing about pigs, hogs or any other farm animal except horses. "Wow!" was all I could say.

Tom and Sue, and several other friends had assembled in the barn yard. Evidently, moving a 400 pound pig from one barnyard to another barnyard was a community project. The distance we had to travel with our less-than-willing pig was about 300 yards. Whit began to instruct those assembled (myself included) in proper pig-moving protocol. Handing each of us a broom or a 2 by 4 foot piece of wood, he indicated that we would form a semi-circle around the pig, banging our wood on the ground and driving the pig forward and across the barnyard. He mentioned that she would be resistant to leaving her own barnyard, where she felt comfortable and safe. (I could see her point of view, as I knew her future involved pork chops!) We were to drive her into the other barnyard, which had a loading chute in the corner. Then she would run up the chute and onto Whit's truck, which was parked against the chute. Once loaded, she would be transported to her final destination.

"Above all," Whit said, "don't let her turn back to her barnyard, or we will have to start all over again." I could have sworn he looked directly at me when he said this! Determined to look like a proper country girl, possibly a future country wife, I vowed then and there to do my part in the pig-loading adventure.

And so we started. Six adults and 1 large pig, shuffling across the barnyard, we probably made a funny picture. Each of us armed with a stick or broom, we tapped the ground loudly, irritating the pig just enough that she began to amble along toward the waiting truck on the other side. Grunting and snuffling, she took her sweet time, pausing now and again to grunt more loudly and peer around at her surroundings.

"She is choosing the weakest link, and she knows it's ME."

By the way, horses generally do not like pigs. I had noticed this fact of life when trail riding with my horses. Pigs could startle even the most placid of equines and I was beginning to understand why. Pigs generally have a strong odor. After all, wallowing in the mud is one of their favorite past-times. They also have beady little eyes (which makes them look exceedingly untrustworthy, if you ask me), a snout which they use for digging in the ground and grunting, which they do a lot of, sometimes loudly and sometimes quietly under their breath.

When we had crossed approximately half of the way, the pig stopped her slow forward progression. Turning around, she glared at each one of our moving crew, in turn. It almost seemed as though she was sizing us up! We all started banging our sticks on the ground and hollering some version of "move it, pig". She was unimpressed, now beginning to understand that we were separating her from her previous home.

Surveying our group, one at a time, she finally fixated those beady eyes on me. "OH, NO," was all I could think! "She is choosing the weakest link, and she knows it's ME."

With a combination of grunts and squeals, this very large pig lowered her head and charged across the barnyard, running straight at me! "Oh no you don't," I yelled. (I did not want Whit to think I was a wimpy pig-drover.) Banging my stick with renewed fervor, I called out loudly, "Turn around you pig. You are not getting past me!"

Despite my yelling like a banshee and my powerful stick beating on the ground, the pig advanced on me. Lowering her head, I think she meant to push me aside. However, I did not yield! She drove her enormous head right between my legs!

The next thing I knew, I was riding a 400 pound pig backwards, bouncing along on her ample back! "Help!" I sputtered, as we charged along. "Help!" I don't know what I expected the rest of the pig-movers to do about my situation, but I certainly did not expect them to be falling on the ground laughing! Covering ground quickly now, I rode that pig, squealing and grunting (both of us), until she took an unscheduled left turn, which deposited me into the barnyard and into the stuff that barnyards are famous for…manure! This was turning out to be quite a date.

When he was able to control his laughing, Whit ambled up to me, offering his hand and brushing off the worst of the smelly stuff now smeared on my jeans. Expecting him to apologize for putting me in grave pig-danger, he calmly deadpanned, "Now, I TOLD you not to let her get past you…"

– Brooke on Pokey

Chapter 4

Pokey the Wonder Pony

"Horses are very intelligent creatures, and emotional sensitivity is something that all intelligent, thinking creatures possess."

Buck Brannaman

"Can you come over, right now? Something is terribly wrong with our pony!" Such was the phone call I received on a beautiful May afternoon, prime lesson time for a riding instructor. The caller was a parent of one of my students, and she sounded genuinely hysterical. First reaction, of course, was to put off a response until a more convenient time, but…Carole's voice was plainly frantic, and I am a horsewoman as well as a teacher.

"Are you sure you need me now? Can it wait? No, well, then I'll be right over."

On the way over to their farm, I mulled over all the different calls I had gotten over the years. Some of these were life and some were death. Some were humorous and some were irritating, some were genuine and some were frivolous. I couldn't help but wonder which kind this would be.

I didn't have to wait long. When I pulled up to the barn, the concerned Mom and her frantic nine year old daughter were waiting, holding "Pokey"—1300 pounds of pony on a frame intended to carry 900 pounds! The setting was gorgeous, forty acres of the best pasture fields in Rockingham County, complete with the lush green grass that comes with spring in Virginia. And Pokey shared that excellent location with a couple of steers. Sounds ideal, except for one thing: Pokey was literally eating himself to death!

There he stood, overweight to the extreme, and completely miserable, developing laminitis and refusing to take even one more unnecessary step. His feet were hot and painful. Without intervention, Pokey's useful life could rapidly come to an end.

> *"Laminitis" in horses is pain and inflammation of the sensitive laminae of the horse's foot or feet.*

For those not familiar with the term, "laminitis" in horses is pain and inflammation of the sensitive laminae of the horse's foot or feet. This can be caused by an imbalance of nutrients or by extreme stress of one nature or another, be it illness, fever, or overeating. Surveying the situation, it was clear that Pokey was overeating, taking in way more nutrients that his body could process. This scenario can lead to the distention of the hoof wall, causing the sole to fall, and the bones on the inside of the foot and leg to be unsupported. In extreme cases, the coffin bone leaves its normal position, rotating inside the hoof wall, and occasionally traveling down through the bottom of the sole. Intense pain results, and the horse or pony must be put out of its misery.

Looking at the stricken faces of the owners, I had to ask several questions. "Have you called the vet? How long has he been like this? Do you understand the term"laminitis"? Are you prepared to take immediate action?" I felt like the bearer of very bad news as I described the condition as I saw it. They were caring horse owners who just didn't see that they were killing Pokey with kindness, and that he was now critical.

Dona and her Mom were shocked and scared when I

explained this to them. Truly they loved this pony (I would come to understand how much and why in the coming years), and they wanted him to be well and happy. So, we made a plan to move him, then and there, to my farm where he could go into the Diet Center (read dry lot), and have his food intake monitored. We consulted a veterinarian regarding medications to lessen his discomfort, and a realistic slim-down program.

Now, you might wonder, what was Pokey's reaction to these life-saving measures? Was he overcome with the equine equivalent of gratitude for our intervention? Absolutely NOT. Horses and ponies are not equipped with a shut-off valve for eating. Grazers by nature, they are driven by the relentless need to eat unceasingly. In the wild, foraging takes up 20 hours of every 24, with the horse constantly searching out the next patch of grass. In the wild, life is good in the warm months (read overeating) and harsh in the cold months (starvation) . But under domesticated circumstances, we take the edge off the searching, providing equines with reasonably consistent food intake. However, they still need to forage and graze, and our lush, fertilized pastures are a vast improvement to the sparse prairie grasses of the undomesticated equine past. Hence, we must be careful not to overfeed.

Pokey had great natural instincts, and after we got him over the immediate crisis, he was determined to go back to his previous eating patterns. We were equally determined to prevent his laminitic condition from recurring. And this is where we discovered another of Pokey's qualities: he was a first rate escape artist. There was not a gate he couldn't open, there was no rope or knot beyond his untying capabilities. He was amazing. And he had a delightful sense of humor. He had an instinct for being in the right place at the right time, and a sense of humor that few equines could match.

One evening, he showed me his sense of humor and his intelligence. I put him into his stall for the evening, limiting his access to grass to a 6 hour period of time each day. During this time he would go out to pasture with five or six other geldings which he loved. By nature quite gregarious, he got along with **almost** all of his buddies. So, having personally put him up for the night, and carefully closing the latch on his door, I left the barn.

Imagine my surprise the next morning when I came out to feed and found Pokey and five geldings wandering around the barn lot!!! Pokey had unlatched his door, and then proceeded to unlatch the doors of his friends from his turn-out area. He had *not* freed the mares and he had *not* freed a horse named Rusty, the only pasture mate that regularly gave him a hard time. Now that was evidence of extreme dexterity and discerning taste, two characteristics not usually attributed to equines. He **knew** how to open the stall doors and he **chose** which other horses to set free!

Funny as this episode was, I knew a challenge when I saw one. How were we going to keep Pokey where we put him? Over the years that I would know him, Pokey kept me challenged and thinking. After the "pony party" incident, we were careful to put a double-ended snap on every door and gate used to contain him. He did not have the benefit of an opposing thumb and finger, and therefore could not operate a snap of this type. Score one for the humans!

> *Never assume anything when dealing with horses, especially creative, smart ones.*

One might wonder how I knew it was Pokey who staged the "pony party" and invited his friends. Well, on several other occasions, I had seen him hang his head out over the dutch door of his stall and play with the latch until he slid it open. But he had settled in and discontinued those efforts, and I assumed he had forgotten about it. One of the lessons which Pokey taught me was this: *never assume anything when dealing with horses, especially creative, smart ones.*

Horses and ponies do not like to be taken for granted. For that matter, who does? If you are casual in this regard, they will certainly show you the error of your ways.

Dona and her Mom were grateful to have their wonderful pony restored to health, and elected to keep him at our farm. Further, we worked out an exchange arrangement, where their expenses for keeping him with me would be reduced in proportion to the lessons he gave to other students, with me as translator. Why the strange terminology? How was I the translator? How did *he* give lessons? Well, the story continues…

We took to calling him *Pokey the Wonder Pony*, alias Hocus Pocus. He was never the fastest guy out of the starting gate. He was never the fanciest mover in his classes at horse shows. He probably wasn't even the best-looking boy his momma ever had. But Pokey did have some qualities besides speed, looks and flash—he had brains, patience and *class*. In our fast-paced world where looks and outstanding talent are rewarded, Pokey might have seemed an anachronism. He looked like an over-grown POA (Pony of the Americas), and moved a little like a washing machine. His talents were definitely not in the packaging. Yet he was a constant source of joy to those who knew him, and I am ever-grateful for the time I spent with him.

I eventually met the trainer who had brought him to our area. He *discovered Pokey* at a killer sale (a sale where horses are often bought for slaughter). This trainer walked by the white pony with brown and black spots, noting his thin and sick condition. "Thin!" I exclaimed. "That was not the Pokey I first met!" Evidently, having suffered from poor care and management under an owner unknown to us, Pokey was sent to this sale, essentially to be killed and turned into some type of feed. My trainer friend said that Pokey, although pitifully thin and sick, held his head up as best he could, looking out at this prospective buyer with a calm and forthright expression. The trainer bought him on a hunch there was more to this underfed equine than most could see—and he was so right.

Dona and her mother bought the rehabilitated Pokey from this trainer after he had been restored to health, vaccinated and evaluated as to suitability for young riders. (Pokey obviously had some "cat" qualities. Seems like he was working on the nine-lives principle.)

Kind beyond measure, Pokey never let anyone fall off who was not absolutely determined to do so. This gift of patience enabled his young riders to spend countless hours grooming, saddling and riding him. Some days I wondered how he could endure it. Tolerance enabled him to ignore bouncing hands and flopping legs.

Young riders are not noted for their body control or their judgment regarding proper riding protocol and technique. Pokey left that part of the teaching plan up to me. He seemed to instinctively know that no one can learn if they are afraid, and so he took seriously the job of putting riders at ease.

Young riders are not noted for their body control or their judgment

As I have previously mentioned, he had a grand sense of humor. He was not above stealing an occasional candy bar or apple from an unsuspecting young equestrian. One day a little boy of 6 or so began wailing loudly, clutching the breast pocket of his shirt with one hand and holding Pokey's reins with the other. I ran to the child, but due to the snuffling and blubbering, I could not make out the nature of the problem. Judging by the body language, it seemed for all the world like Pokey was being accused of biting this little guy! "Did Pokey bite you," I inquired, hardly able to believe such a thing even as I voiced it.

"No," the little boy cried, "but he did steal my Reese's Cup out of my pocket!" I looked at Pokey, as he calmly finished swallowing the candy bar, paper and all. I swear, you could almost see him smiling. Partly out of relief and partly out of the sheer hilarity of the situation, the boy's mother and I began to laugh. This of course only made the little guy cry all the harder, as it seemed the adults did not appreciate the seriousness of this crime.

That was Pokey in a nutshell. He was kind and generous, but certainly not beyond a trick or two, usually out-maneuvering his human friends. After Dona outgrew him, I purchased him for permanent residence in my lesson program. He proved to be invaluable. He taught several generations of students, with young parents bringing their own small children to sit on his safe back. "This is the famous Pokey," they would explain to the eager little faces. "He taught me to ride."

Pokey had a well-rounded career. He was interviewed on television (he tried to eat the microphone of the reporter). He gave countless horsemanship demonstrations at elementary schools and PTA fund-raisers (he could always be counted on to remain calm in crowded situations). I loaned him one day per week to the local riding-for-the-handicapped program (he loved those children). And he was a tremendous asset to our riding program, as I have previously written.

On a more personal note, I eventually became a mother in my own right. Pokey's kindness and steady nature allowed both of my daughters to ride and show when they were quite tiny. He would enter the ring, take the rail and hold his ground, following the commands of the announcer, with or without human assistance.

On one memorable afternoon at our farm, my oldest daughter, Diana, was riding Pokey in the ring. I was close-by, working on barn chores. We had an agreement, Diana and I. She was only four years old, and she was to keep her riding to walk, and trot, unless directly supervised by me.

Things seemed to be going well, until I heard her voice encouraging Pokey, "You can do it, boy, you can do it!" This alarmed me, as it did not seem appropriate encouragement for a sedate ride in the ring. I ran from the barn just in time to see Pokey cantering toward a large jump, his eyes wild with terror and apprehension. On his back was my courageous four year old, beating him with a riding crop (where did that come from?), and goading him into high gear. "You can do it, boy!"

I feared impending disaster, and Pokey had the good sense to feel it too. Trying to keep the fear out of my voice, I called to him, just as I often did in lessons. Would he hear me? Would my voice, from a distance, be enough to countermand the urgings of his rider and the fear in his eyes? Would he listen to me rather than obey the commands of his demanding little jockey? Would he recognize the danger she was in, and would he help me save her?

You bet! Pokey stopped in his tracks, quickly, but not so quickly as to unseat his precious cargo. While he and I both breathed a sigh of relief, Diana expressed her disappointment in no uncertain terms. "He can do it, Momma, and so can I!" she exclaimed. "Yes," I responded, but you'll have to wait until you're, ummm, five…" I hugged the ever-sensible Pokey, telling him just how much I loved him. But I think he already knew.

Learning to post up and down on a trotting horse is a beginner task.

By the time my second child was ready to ride, Pokey was getting to be a senior citizen. Still, he had good health and the proper amount of energy for teaching what we in the horse business refer to as "up-down" lessons. Learning to post up and down on a trotting horse is a beginner task. It takes a horse or pony with a slow, steady rhythm to enable folks with marginal balance, a little fear and no skill at all to be able to learn such things. Pokey was just the guy for the job.

One day at a horse competition, I sent my second child, Brooke (you guessed it—age four), into a walk, trot and canter class, pony pleasure I think it was. Her legs were barely long enough to straddle Pokey's still substantial girth. But she had grit, determination and the burning desire to show and compete. There were spectators there that day who felt that I was a bit remiss in my motherly concern to let such a young rider compete in a ring full of children and ponies. But, my faith in Pokey was great. Time and again he had proven himself to be sensible and generous of spirit.

Fifteen children entered the ring that day, on an assortment of ponies. The children ranged in age from four (mine) to 15 or so, and the ponies were grey, black, bay and chestnut, in various sizes. Around they went, at the direction of the announcer. First at a walk, then a trot and finally---be still my heart---the canter was called. Fifteen children on ponies began to canter. Suddenly, as can happen when large equines are being piloted by small children, one of the ponies went out of control, his little rider struggling mightily to guide him. The black pony began to buck and bounce around, and then tossed his young rider onto the ground. This was not a good development for the rider and it was not a good development for Brooke and Pokey, for the dislodged child had fallen directly onto the path in front of Pokey!

With Brooke's short legs, any rapid sideways movement would unseat her. On the other hand, Pokey knew he wasn't supposed to run over anyone. The safety of two children, one on the ground and one on his back, depended on Pokey's reaction. This posed a rather daunting dilemma for an equine. The crowd issued a collective gasp, and my own heart nearly stopped. Luckily, Pokey had seen this situation developing. *He* had a plan. Without missing a beat, he maneuvered off the ring rail, cantered smoothly around the fallen angel, and continued his canter until the announcer called for a halt. As the riders and ponies lined up in the center of the ring, I stood at the gate beaming proudly as Brooke and Pokey were awarded their blue ribbon. A few minutes later, a distinguished gentleman who had witnessed this incident approached me, checkbook in hand. "I need this pony, Pokey is it, for my grandchild. He is priceless. Money is no object. Just tell me how much."

I looked up at him, looked over at Pokey and Brooke and the answer was obvious. "Thanks for the kind offer, but I guess you said it all. He will never be for sale. Pokey is *priceless.*"

– Diana Riding Pokey

The years went by, and Pokey continued his career as lesson pony, show pony for the beginner riders, and safe mount for anyone lucky enough to have the opportunity to ride him. He also continued to play occasional tricks on his caretakers. He untied ropes intended to hold him, he sampled more than a few flowers, stole a few candies here and there, and he raised more than a few children.

One spring, when Pokey was thirty years of age, he began to lose weight and look less than his usual healthy self. After several diagnostic visits from Dr. Don Cromer, the dedicated veterinarian who had helped me care for him all those years, it was determined that he had an inoperable thyroid tumor. Only slightly visible from the outside of his throat, this tumor was growing on the inside, slowly but surely blocking Pokey's ability to eat and swallow, and would eventually compromise his breathing. Dr. Cromer gently informed me that Pokey's last days were approaching. It was up to me to decide what to do. After much soul-searching, I decided that when Pokey became unable to breathe comfortably, we would have the veterinarian put him to sleep, and bury him next to the paddock where he and his buddies had run and played and grazed.

The day came all too soon. Our family, both girls now grown to teen age, walked Pokey down to the chosen location. We coddled and pet him, with Dr. Cromer, from the Westwood Animal Clinic, waiting patiently for us to say our good-byes. I am ever-grateful for the help and concern of this gentle veterinarian, who clearly understands that caring for animals means caring for their humans as well. His medical advice and treatment for our horses has always been careful and meticulous, and his kindness and generosity of spirit has made the hard days more bearable for the human clients.

Coming down the hill to his final resting place, Pokey tried to graze along the way, but could not really swallow. Still that wonderful, indomitable spirit of his prevailed. He had a sparkle in his eye….. and I had a Reese's Cup in my hand. I gave him his last candy bar, as the vet administered the massive dose of heart-stopping medication. Down he went, sinking onto the green grass that he loved so well.

"Old man," I said to him, as I watched him taking his last breaths, "I think you've finally used up your nine lives on this earth. But I think I'll see you again one day. I love you." And through my own tears, I think I saw him smile.

Chapter 5

Cheeseburger in Paradise

"You can tell a horse owner by the interior of their car. Boots, mud, manure, straw, items of tack, and a screwed-up waxed jacket of incredible antiquity. There is normally a top layer of children and dogs."

Helen Thompson

The setting for the stories which follow is the scenic Shenandoah Valley. It is truly beautiful here. In the spring, the birds are plentiful, waking me in the mornings with their songs. The crocuses cannot wait to burst forth from the earth, often peeking out before the last snow is finally gone. The summers are quite steamy, but here on our hill, the breeze always prevails. The smell of new mown hay is often in the wind, along with a few whiffs of poultry houses, as we are the poultry capital of the world. Fall, oh the Fall, is my favorite, with colors that take your breath away. Gold and red, brown and green, the trees are so beautiful as they change. I find Autumn intriguing, opening the door to introspection and reflection. The winters, last but not least, are often surprising, wavering between 65 and 12, and all temperatures in between. Often just a few days separates the huge fluctuations in temperature and precipitation, and, as they say, "if you don't like the weather now, just wait five minutes…"

That said, I would be remiss if I didn't describe life on the farm, particularly our farm. If you live on a farm, or are close to "farm friends", the following chapter may not surprise you. But if you are a nice, organized, city person, maybe this will help you understand your country friends, or at least make you more tolerant of the peculiar things that happen when you visit them.

Animal must come first

It must be said that anyone who has animals knows the animal must come first. They do not have the capability, in the domesticated setting, to search out food and water for themselves. Therefore, we must provide for them. And their most dire and demanding needs always happen when your household is going crazy.

Case in point would be the fourth birthday of my youngest child. She was very excited to have friends and relatives over to celebrate, so I, in a fit of motherly zeal, offered to make dinner for a mere twenty (20!) of our nearest and dearest. That in itself wasn't so very daunting. My husband and I both come from large families, and we are used to such gatherings. The complicating factor was this: one of the broodmares was overdue for foaling, and I had been getting up every two to three hours for many days, trying to make sure she was well and having no birthing difficulties. As luck, or lack of same, would have it, this mother decided to have her foal at four a. m. on Sunday morning, the day of the birthday gathering. The birth goes well, and we, as a family, feel excited the new arrival shares a birthday with our daughter. She, in fact, thinks that this is wonderful because I woke her and her sister, at their request, so they could witness the birth.

After the new foal was on the ground, daughters one and two went on back to bed, while Mom waited to see junior have his first meal, give him a tetanus vaccination, and be sure his mom passed her placenta. (That's right, farm life is not for wimps.) Then I laid down, boots and all, and fell into a coma-like sleep, for one hour. Soon, oh so soon, it was time for breakfast. A quick shower, a cup of coffee, and a few smiley eggs later (you know, bread cut into smiley faces with egg poured in, *very* special), we are out feeding the troops, twenty-five horses, eight cats and five dogs. Feeding the horses, leading them to their paddocks, filling water troughs, putting hay in all paddocks, *starting* the stall cleaning process, all this takes about four hours. (It actually takes about three hours without the help of my four year old birthday girl and her seven and a half year old sister. But, you know, they try to help and I love them for it.)

Now we are up to noon of the birthday celebration, and I am feeling rather self-satisfied. I have "birthed a baby", so to speak, made a special breakfast for the human birthday girl, finished a big part of the farm chores for the day, and am on schedule for cooking the birthday cake and dinner. However, in my life, self-satisfied never lasts long, so I never have to worry about getting conceited or over-confident. My life has a way of keeping me humble, waiting for the next shoe to drop, and so it did. While I am fixing the birthday cake, my youngest runs into the kitchen, "Come quick, Mom, Merry is having her puppies."

– Boston Terrier Puppies

You guessed it, the purebred Boston Terrier, the apple of my eye, has decided to have her babies a day early, and scarcely an hour and a half before the birthday guests are due to arrive! Hooray! Merry is racing around the laundry room, a puppy dangling from her backside, frantic that some foreign object is chasing her. Brooke, the birthday girl is fascinated by the whole spectacle, while the seven year old Diana is shouting instructions and questions. "Help her, Mom. Don't let her drag her baby around. Do all mothers do this? How come all that stuff is coming out?"

Calming the children, I sit upon the floor with the dog, who deposits the puppy in my lap. Wow! That was almost a crisis. Now we have one healthy baby Boston. I reinstall mother and pup in to the previously prepared whelping box, and get up to wash my hands and work on dinner once more. (Yes, I'm being as sanitary as is humanly possible, considering the situation.) Suddenly, wailing resumes. "Mom, she's doing it again!" Brooke and Diana now are panic-stricken unison. "Help, help, she's running around again." Turns out, Merry the dog won't stay in the whelping box unless I stay with her. This would not be a problem, except for-----you guessed it----the birthday.

Brooke looks at me with sad little eyes, "Guess the birthday is canceled, right Mom?" she queries. I would love to say yes, but I just can't. I couldn't bear to disappoint that sweet face. "Of course not. It's just a very special birthday! Just think how *lucky* we are to have so many babies born on your day, Brooke. We have a new baby horse ('it's called a *foal*, Mom, 'she says.) And we have new baby puppies...What a really special day this is." I say, as convincingly as I can. Diana, the oldest and ever practical, says, "This might be a good time to call Granny!"

Reinforcements! Now that's an idea...

CB&O

Farm life is never the same two days in a row, and is never boring. Some of my city relatives and friends have the amazing and inaccurate idea that farm life is pastoral, relaxing and predictable. "Wish I could live on the farm to escape all the stress of my life!" Several of my friends have said these words to me, and I reply with what I hope passes for a beatific smile.

Obviously they have never had a tired, cold and wet husband deposit a baby calf (125 pounds) into an old playpen in their kitchen. This particular baby chose to be born on the coldest day of the year, and my husband left him with the children and I to warm him up. He needed to go out and tend to the cow, who was having difficulties.

"What if he jumps out of the playpen?" I queried. "Relax," was the reply, "he's was too weak and cold. We'll be lucky if we don't lose him." And with that, the husband was gone. The children were thrilled. I focused on cooking supper, while the occupant of the playpen became warmer and drier thanks to an old beauty shop hairdryer, often pressed into service on such occasions.

The smells of steak and biscuits began to fill the room, the table was almost set, and I began to have hope for a quiet evening meal. Just then, squeals of laughter rang out and a loud thump followed. "He's out, Mom, he's out!" yelled the girls. Turning around I discovered the little (!) dude sliding across my kitchen floor, leaving a muddy trail. Quickly I tried to grab him, which only served to alarm him into bawling his complaints to the world. Grabbing his middle, I tried to lift him back into the pen, but he was now so alarmed that all four legs were kicking in different directions. The girls tried to help at this point, and finally we were able to put him back in the pen, which seemed to be the place for him, however temporarily.

I quickly came to the conclusion that semi-clean would no longer apply.

Crisis averted, I thought. Then I looked at each smiling girl, previously semi-clean. (The opposite of semi-clean is semi-dirty, which is the pessimist's view of the same condition.) Glancing down at my own clothing, I quickly came to the conclusion that semi-clean would no longer apply. All three of us were covered in streaks of mud and baby calf slobber; I might also offer that all three of us were fairly smelly as well. Odors of barn, cow and burning steak—yes, that's right, the steak had become a little neglected—now filled the room. At this point, I could either laugh or cry...or yell. The children looked at me, wondering which way this would go. I could feel something bubbling up from deep inside of me, something strong and powerful and potentially loud. When it burst out, laughter (thank God) filled the room, and soon all three of us were sitting on the floor, screaming and laughing and snorting, you know, the sound you make when your laughter takes your breath away.

Trying to get myself under control, I rushed to salvage the steak, which now seemed a bit cannibalistic, considering that we were struggling to save a junior member of the bovine set while cooking one of his distant relatives for dinner. This irony was not lost on the oldest of my girls, who was seven and now asking if we would ever make steaks out of *this* baby. At this juncture, my husband walked in, and I was saved, for the moment.

Covered head to toe in mud, he was recognizable only by his brown eyes, which reflected both concern and relief. "The cow's o. k. How's the little guy?" He asks me. "Just fine, and he is quite a good jumper," I answer. Instructing him to wait by the door, I brought two big towels and instructions. "Take off *everything,* leave it by the door and go straight to the shower! We'll have dinner when you are warm and clean." There's just something unexplainably wonderful about a man with such a big and dedicated heart, albeit a little mud splattered.

I cleaned up the girls and myself, somewhat, and we all met for a dinner that was very short on culinary perfection, but long on the stuff that really counts. Farm life, while not exactly stress-free, certainly provided us with great stories and memories, and times when working together as a family was sweeter than any gourmet dessert, and much better for the heart and soul.

Chapter 6

Stewball

Old Stewball was a racehorse, and I wish he was mine,
He never drank water, he only drank wine.
His bridle was silver, his mane it was gold.
The worth of his saddle has never been told.

I still smile when I think of these lyrics by Peter, Paul and Mary. Their Stewball was quite different than mine. However, my little Stewball left a legacy too, with multiple little children. Standing 12. 1 hands high, this Stewie was adorable, jet black, with a big white star on his forehead. His coat was glossy, his eyes were large and beautiful, his little legs straight and strong. Conformationally speaking, he really was a lovely pony.

Stewball was purchased by some members of our hunt club, with the intention of using him as a "grandchild" pony. They had been led to believe, by the sellers, that this three year old pony would be *perfect* for their purposes. However, Stewie at three was the original "pony from hell". He bucked, he reared, he ran away, in fact I think he spent lots of time thinking up his next pony prank. In effect, he was NOT the perfect pony.

These hunt club grandparents offered to sell me this little gem for a mere $400, assuring me that he *would* be a gem once his quirks were worked out. The end of the story is: they were right! But we had a few bumps on the road to success.....

— Angela and Stewball

So, Stewie came home to my farm, and became my next project. The first day of riding was the stuff of "Funniest Home Video". In fact, I wish now that we had made that video. Probably should have, too, since the $10,000 winner's fee could have paid for a much-needed increase in my health insurance. Anyway, Stewie stood absolutely still until I had completely mounted. How nice, I thought, he's going to be cooperative. NOT! As soon as I had both feet in the stirrups, Stewie began to buck. And he was really good at it. Stewie could have been the Pabst Blue Ribbon bucking champ if only he had been 15 hands tall.

He bucked, dropping his head between his knees. He twisted, changing directions as fast as he could. I don't know how I stayed on, since a 12 hand pony doesn't have much neck to stick out in front of a 5'6" woman. Perhaps it was because I feared to fall off under those thundering little feet. I wasn't about to tell my friends that I had been speared and smeared by a tiny demon. No way!

When he took a breather from all this hard work, I jumped off and got a riding crop, something I could use to even the odds for round two. Stewie saw this and rolled his eyes dramatically, mentally calculating his next round of tricks. Still, he stood quietly for me to remount, as though he felt honor-bound to play by some set of unwritten rules.

Round two was much like round one, with one exception: every time Stewie bucked, I soundly smacked his butt with my crop. When went around the riding arena, buck-smack, buck-smack, buck-smack. His stamina was amazing! Sometime during this lovely process, a good friend of mine had arrived at the barn. I did not see Sue till I heard her laughing. Actually, she was leaning against the ring rail HOWLING. "You look like Calamity Jane", she managed to choke out between gales of laughter. I didn't have time to think of a clever retort, since I was a little preoccupied.

Eventually, Stewie made the connection between bucking and getting spanked with my stick. At the end of round two, he made a cantering pass around the arena without bucking once. Progress comes in small steps, but this seemed like a good place to stop for the day.

In Stewie's defense, I will say that he had equal amounts of smarts and stubbornness. In the next few days, he decided that bucking just wasn't as much fun as he had originally thought, and so he gave it up. You know, I can't remember a time after that first week that he EVER bucked again. He had tried it, found it less than satisfactory, and he let it go.

Being a very clever little fellow, he decided that if bucking was not appreciated then he would develop another little trick for my fun and amusement. Our next ride featured his newest gambit. Trotting around the arena, I felt just great. The sun was warm, the birds were singing, and my little pony project was progressing nicely, or so I thought. Horses rarely give us time to sit on our laurels. While I was in "laurel-land", Stewie showed me his new trick. In mid- stride he stood straight up, front hooves pawing the air like a miniature Lipizzaner stallion. Caught by surprise, I slid off the back, and landed (you guessed it) square on my laurels! Clearly he had out-planned me! At this point I nick-named him "Alpo", after the popular dog food. Not that I would really send him in that direction, but just the thought was comforting to me as I rubbed my back side.

Gathering myself up, including my ego which was being soundly trounced, I remounted. Again he trotted off peacefully enough, then up he went. This time, however, I rapped the top of his head with my crop. He dropped to the ground, startled. We set off at the trot once again, and again he reared straight into the air. Now, I want you to picture this: 12 hand pony, 5'6" rider, no neck to lean on. Whenever this pony reared, I leaned forward on his neck. I didn't want to over balance him and make him topple over to the rear, but when I leaned up his neck, my head was over the top of his head! The ridiculousness of this picture was not lost on me, but if Stewie was indeed to be a good children's pony, these tricks could not prevail. So, up he went, and I popped him on the top of his head with my crop. Dropping to the ground, Stewie appeared to be studying on this new development. To my recollection, he only tried this one more time, and then rearing when the same route as bucking. A quick study, he decided it was not in his best interest to continue those two bad habits.

> *A quick study, he decided it was not in his best interest to continue those two bad habits.*

After a few more weeks of riding him myself, I decided to let one of my more self-assured beginner students give him the kid test. Angie, a little horse-crazy dynamo wanted to be the first child to ride Stewball. Keeping a hand on the reins, I helped her mount. Still not convinced, I was just as apprehensive as Angela was excited. Lo and behold, the little guy was wonderful. After a few trips around the ring, I let her go and they had the first of many wonderful rides.

Stewball was becoming a wonderful pony. Smart and creative, he was fun to have around. Within months, he was well on his way to becoming a great lesson pony, and we were taking him to horse shows and trail rides. Angie in particular felt that he could do no wrong. Although he was cute and more reliable than not, I wouldn't exactly say that he could do no wrong.

There was the evening, when out with four other horses and ponies for a trail ride, when he got spooked by some children popping out from beneath a tree. All of the horses startled a bit. Stewie startled a lot. Looking for escape, he plowed headfirst into a field of standing corn, totally disappearing. Being so small, and carrying an 8 year old child, he completely disappeared in the leaves. The mother of the child, Sue, looked at me with terror on her face. "How will we find them," she asked calmly, trying not to appear panic-stricken. For two or three minutes, I pondered an answer to that question, having never encountered this particular problem before. Walking along the edge of the corn field, suddenly we heart a great rustling in the field. Angie and Stewie burst forth, with Angie wearing the biggest of grins. "Now *that* was fun, she shouted." I felt a few of my hairs turn grey, but all was well.

Then, of course, we have the day at the Sacred Heart show grounds, in Winchester, Virginia. The pony ring was bordered by snow fencing, with no gates at either the entrance or exit. Knowing Stewie's proclivity for creative thinking, I almost canceled the pony classes for him. Being really concerned that he would regard the lack of in and out gates as an opportunity to leave the ring at will, I did not want him to embarrass Angela with a hasty retreat during her over- fences round. Angela was a plucky little thing, however, so she convinced me to let her try. Attempting to stack the odds in her favor, I stationed myself at one of the openings to the ring, and I asked her parents to block the other opening.

Holding my breath, I watched as Stewie and Angela started their warm-up circle. They were beautiful, good pace, good rhythm. Straight to fence one, the little jockey rode him down the line to fence two, going away from the in-gate opening. As they turned to come down the line of jumps on the other side of the arena, I saw a glint in Stewie's eye. Jumping fence three in fine form, our little prankster took hold of the bit, and hit a new gear, flying over fence four and heading straight for the out-gate opening. Standing in that location, I began waving my arms and shouting at him to stop. I called him names, I made rude references to his parentage, and I did not move out of the opening. *He* did not falter. Putting his head down, he hit me hard in the shoulder and plowed on through!

Disappearing for a moment into the sparse crowd, he emerged charging straight for the other ring opening! With Angela grinning all the way, he returned to the ring, and finished the course! I was grateful that no one was hurt, but I was mad as a hornet at his antics. The judge, however, found Angie's pluck quite charming, and invited her back into the ring for an honorable mention.

Mentioning the bad-boy events, I must also tell of his good deeds. One such day occurred at the WeyersCave Horse Show. The sky was growing ever darker, and it seemed that we would be getting a summer thundershower. During the pony under saddle class, there came a tremendous clap of thunder, amplified by the public address system, as the lightning ran in on the electrical cords. The announcer, sitting up on a podium and holding the microphone, was blown off his chair, and the loud clap was enhanced by the microphone. Running toward the announcer, I stopped in my tracks. "That man is already dead," I thought. "Better to save the children."

I ran into the pony ring, where twelve little ponies were galloping in twelve different directions. Children were crying, parents and trainers were trying to find their riders, and the rain came in a downpour. Wading through the mayhem, I helped several wide-eyed children off of their panic stricken ponies, all the while trying to find Angie and Stewie.

Finally I sighted them, standing calmly in the middle of the ring! Stewie was waiting stoically, calmly watching the craziness around him. "Angela," I choked out, "where have you been?" With all of the innocence and courage an eight year old can muster, she said, "Me and Stewie were waiting for you." "Good job, you two," I managed to sputter, "Now let's get out of here!"

Leave it to Stewie to be on his best behavior in a crisis. By the way, the storm passed but the announcer lived! After being treated by the emergency squad, the stalwart fellow climbed back up onto his podium and began to announce the remainder of the show! Gotta love those horse show folks, tough as nails and twice as sturdy…

Another feather in Stewie's proverbial hat was earned when he was helping out the Therapeutic riding program in our area. Being in the start-up phase, this group had neither horses nor facility, so, for a time, I lent them several of our lesson horses and they met at our farm on Friday afternoons. By now, Stewie had mellowed into a reasonably decent fellow, so he was one of the equines used in the program.

Stewie was hitched to a post and a young girl with spina bifida was leaning on him, giving him a good grooming. Unable to walk without her crutches, she had laid them down in order to use her hands to groom the pony. Another young man walked by their location, where he lost his balance and fell down behind the tied pony. Having a balance and coordination issue, this young man fell often and he was not hurt or alarmed. I, however, was having a heart attack! As he fell, directly behind the pony and making lots of noise, his head landed directly between the pony's back legs!

I will be really disappointed if there is no place in Heaven for ponies and horses.

Time stopped…or so it seemed. Trying not to spook Stewie (remember that he is holding up the girl), I suggested that the young man stand up as soon as possible. Understatement of the year, but I was trying not to alarm the girl, the pony or the fallen boy. Any moment could bring disaster, because if Stewie kicked, or even took a step, a severe head injury could result. But if I pulled the pony away, the girl would fall down beside him, possibly sustaining an injury too. Stewie chose that very moment to look at me. "Chill out," he seemed to say. "I've got this covered."

And so he did! Never moving a muscle, he waited patiently for the young man to stand up. Being physically challenged but desiring to be independent, the boy would not accept my help as he struggled to regain his feet. His body was slow, but he had lots of personal gumption. Rising to his feet, he careened away.

The girl went on brushing Stewie and I knew then and there that Stewie would one day arrive in Heaven. I will be really disappointed if there is no place in Heaven for ponies and horses. There must certainly be a place for them, for they make our lives so much more meaningful while we are here on earth. They are, after all, a gift from God. Certainly, Stewie had earned his place.

The years went by, Angela grew up, and countless other children rode on this clever little pony. Eventually, I sold him to a young father for his little son, and kind of lost track of him. But I will never forget him, the good, the bad, the ugly and the beautiful. He was quite a character, and he certainly taught me a lot about smart ponies.

Chapter 7

Princess Cocoa

"Be wary of the horse with a sense of humor."

Pam Brown

"She won't canter!" Such was my introduction to Cocoa. Her owners, a nice couple with two young children, seemed pleased with her in every other way. "She's beautiful, sweet, kind, gentle, and perfect for our children, but she won't canter! Will you work with her?" asked Lynne. Now Lynne and Perlie had owned horses most of their lives, but a little pony was certainly a different experience when compared to 16 hand horses. Just smelling grain could put five pounds on her, and pony personalities are quite different from their larger horse cousins. So, this young couple was at wits end trying to get some level of performance out of this little gal.

Being young and hungry, I readily agreed to train Cocoa for a few weeks. How hard could it be to train a small, 10 year old pony? Later that afternoon she arrived—all 12 hands of her. And she was a sight for sore eyes. The reason for her lack of forward momentum was readily apparent. On her 12 hand frame she was easily carrying 750 pounds! I had my work cut out for me.

The little pinto mare looked like a barrel on pegs, but she had a princess attitude. She knew her rights and she fully intended to exercise them. And that was about all she intended to exercise. But I had given my word, so now began the task of turning Cocoa into a useful citizen. Into the diet paddock she went, grumbling all the way. No blade of grass could be found in her dry lot, no treats would be offered. Her human family took great offense at this, but I convinced them that this was in Cocoa's best interests. No grain, high in calories and sugar, would be offered. She was to have lots of clean fresh water, and small quantities of hay to meet her needs for roughage. And while she was dieting, we would begin her training.

She instantly hated me, and, at first, refused to be caught, staying just out of reach in her paddock. I would walk toward her, she would retreat. Her disdain was clear. So, on the second evening of her visit to my farm, I sat down next to her allotment of hay and waited.

I brushed her and spoke gently, hoping to make friends

Eventually, hunger got the best of her, and she huffed her way up the hill to check out the dinner menu. Cocoa sniffed the flake of hay, stomped her foot and waddled away, insulted. Me, I waited, counting on her growling stomach to override her gourmet pallet. I felt certain she would come back. After two hours and much consternation, the little mare did return. And while she grudgingly munched her hay, I brushed her and spoke gently, hoping to make friends in this way.

By the third day, I could walk up to her. She allowed herself to be caught, and then began phase two of her training. Leading her to the barn, I selected saddle and bridle. Tacking up was no problem, but getting the saddle to stay in place on a body that round was nearly impossible.

Mounting up, I felt like Calamity Jane. I am 5'6" tall, and Cocoa was 12 hands tall and wide, so we made quite a picture. As I mounted, the saddle shifted completely sideways. Cocoa took great delight in this and twirled away as fast as she could. She looked rather like the dancing hippo in the Disney movie Fantasia. Saddle hanging under her belly, the little brown and white bombshell proceeded to trot around the arena, obviously delighted that she had been victorious in Round One.

Dusting myself off and saying a few words I won't repeat here, I eventually caught the little scamp and tried again. Pulling up the girth so tight I was sure I was squeezing the very breath out of her, I again climbed aboard. Time stood still—and so did Cocoa. She plainly refused to take even one step. No attempt to coax her forward yielded any result. I attempted to turn right, then left. I coaxed, then I kicked, then I cussed. Still she refused to budge an inch. Finally, in desperation, I went to my stick. The moment my crop struck her ample derriere, the fireworks began.

How could anything so overweight buck so well! Kicking and bucking every step of the way, Cocoa expressed her contempt for work in any form. She had no work ethic, and she resisted developing one with all her might. Around the ring we went, stick, buck, kick, trot. After twenty minutes or so of this strange routine, we were both wringing wet and hopping mad. I stopped for the day, fearful that one or both of us might suffer a heart attack.

So it went for a few more days. Cocoa slowly and grudgingly began to slim down with gentle (gentle?) exercise and a controlled diet. By the end of week two, she had lost 30 pounds or so. It was time to introduce the canter. I tacked up, putting on saddle and bridle as usual, tugging up the girth as tight as I dared. I really didn't want the saddle to turn again. We went through our usual walk and trot workout. She was improving! Still carrying my stick, I used it less frequently. Cocoa was becoming a little more willing.

After about twenty minutes, I asked for the canter. Time again stood still, and so did Cocoa. She had read the fine print in her contract, and nowhere did it say "canter"! That was just way too much work, and she wasn't having any. When all other forms of encouragement failed, I once again resorted to my riding crop, issuing the verbal command, "Canter!"

In the twinkling of an eye---her's---she dropped her head, bucked like a bronc, and then threw herself into reverse faster than I would have believed possible. Once again, I found myself sitting in the dirt, sweating and using my new vocabulary. Cocoa won Round Two.

After she finished gloating, or at least it seemed so, I caught her and climbed aboard. Having experienced her evasive maneuvers, I was at least a little more prepared. A small pony has a very short neck, and my torso was longer. When she dropped her head to the ground, there just wasn't anything out in front of me. Asking for canter, I popped her with my crop, and she did the stop, drop and buck thing. But this time, I stuck on!

Every time she bucked I tapped her with my crop

Every time she bucked I tapped her with my crop, an eight inch slender piece of wood with a flapping leather end on it, more insult than injury to a 750 pound equine. An attention getter, this device called a crop or "stick" is supposed to encourage an equine to travel forward, a direction which this wayward little pony disliked with a vengeance.

Finally, she broke into a rollicking canter. I felt rather like I was on a ship at sea. We went twice around the arena, and the little overweight pony was quite winded. Returning to the walk, we changed direction, walking a little more as I praised her for her efforts. Then, after she had rested, I asked for the canter again. Stop, drop, buck, pop! Around and around we went, and then… she cantered.

Another week went by, and we continued our strange love-hate relationship. Brushing and feeding she accepted from me gratefully and almost happily. Working she did grudgingly, but with ever increasing stamina.

At the end of five weeks, Cocoa had lost a cool 80 or 90 pounds, and could canter for short stretches on command, without bucking! Her owners were well pleased, and happily paid me my fee, $225. 00. (Remember, this was in the late 1970's.)

As luck would have it, the owners were so pleased that they weekly brought me Cocoa and their children, Scott and Amanda. I taught the pony and the children together until they outgrew each other. Cocoa provided them with lots of good pony experiences, and while she was never totally cooperative, she was safe and made riding fun. She was never dangerous, and was genuinely affectionate with children, always preferring children to adults. She continued to regard me with suspicion, and grudging respect. She did her work passably well, and her children loved riding her. That was good enough for me.

– Dana riding Princess Cocoa

As time went by, these children grew too tall for her and moved on to faster, taller mounts. One day, Lynne, the mother of the children and Cocoa's owner, brought her to my barn, and kindly put her into my program. "You did a good job with Cocoa and our children, so my husband and I would like to give her to you for your lesson program." Cocoa looked at me as if to say "What do you think about that? Just remember, *I am the Princess.*"

Years passed, and Cocoa did indeed prove herself useful in teaching children to ride. She was more careful with them than she was with adults, and preferred their company.

My veterinarian has always helped me keep my horses well with excellent health care. Little Princess Cocoa was somewhat of a treatment challenge, however, as she hated vaccinations. All lesson animals on my farm must be vaccinated for rabies, influenza and the like, so Dr. Don Cromer and I set about the task of immunizing Cocoa. I went into her stall, put on her halter, and walked her out into the aisle way. She took one look at him, and took off for the door, dragging me as I held fast to the rope. "Hang on and I'll help you," he called. Grabbing on to the end of the rope with me, we both dug in our feet, and she continued to tow us through the dirt, like awkward water skiers. Finally getting her stopped, we put her back into her stall, slammed the door closed, and watched her race around the 12 by 12 foot enclosure, mad as a hornet. Then we both burst into laughter! "Now what," I asked? "We've got to vaccinate her, but I don't think we can hold her."

He thoughtfully regarded the angry little pony, and then devised a plan. We pulled the lead rope still tied to her halter through the bars of the stall and fastened the rope to the stout middle pole, effectively short-snubbing her to the pole. Then he approached her with syringe in hand. Steam poured from her ears, or so it seemed. Every muscle was tense as he deftly slipped the needle into the muscled area of her neck. Reacting, she swung her body as far as she could, smashing the needle and syringe in his hand. "Okay for you, K. P.," he said. "Now we have to do this again." The next try was successful, thankfully, and as he was leaving I asked him what the K. P. stood for. Was it some form of endearment (ho, ho), a new technical term, veterinary terminology with which I was unfamiliar? Dr. Cromer has a great smile and a dry sense of humor. Grinning at me, he said "K. P. stands for "Killer Pony", and that's what she thinks she is. I'm just grateful that she doesn't weigh 700 pounds!" (I didn't say a word…)

When Cocoa was 20 years old, I decided to give her to my sister, Judy, for her children, who were ages five, three, and one. Cocoa, except for her continuing aversion to vets, was kind to children, and had certainly mellowed out with age. I told Judy that this pony was no spring chicken, but probably had a few good years left. And that she did.

Cocoa raised these little girls, letting them ride and learn on her always-ample back. Because Cocoa never did prefer to go fast (except if you carried a crop), she could be trusted to amble around the ring with these tiny riders. She was the entertainment at many birthday parties, gave horse demonstrations at the children's school, and was always a community attraction. She loved little children, letting them lead her around, and even gave pony rides to the dog.

One afternoon, Judy's youngest child, Alicia, returned from the barn, carrying Cocoa's bridle over her shoulder. Judy inquired about the riding experience of the day, to which the 6 year old exclaimed, "You know, Mom, Cocoa goes where Cocoa wants!" I think that about says it all.

On one memorable occasion, Cocoa was given a starring role in the church Christmas play. She was to be the little donkey that would carry Mary and Joseph into Bethlehem. As everyone knows, donkeys have much longer ears than Princess ponies. So some ear extensions were constructed to make Cocoa look her part. We will never know if it was the cold weather, the long wait until she was to go on stage, or the long floppy ears. Perhaps Cocoa harbored some politically incorrect notion of ponies being vastly superior to donkeys. Whatever the reason, Cocoa began to paw her hay in the manger. She stomped her hooves, and shook her head. She glared at the audience with malevolence completely out of tune with the Christmas season.

– Alicia and Princess Cocoa

At the appointed time, my sister took the children who were to play Mary and Joseph by the hand. "Time to mount up and ride into Bethlehem!" she told them. The doors to the sanctuary opened and the faces of the waiting congregation could be seen. Little "Mary" (a six year old from the congregation) had been watching all of Cocoa's gyrations. Looking at the irate Cocoa, still stomping and shaking and glaring, "Mary" responded in a loud, clear voice that *easily* carried into the church where eager parents and friends waited. "Ummm, no thanks," Mary said. "Me and Joseph, we'll be WALKING!"

It brought down the house!

Cocoa went on to raise those three little girls, half the neighborhood, and then, when these children were in high school and college, Judy adopted a little boy, Joey. Cocoa, now 38 years old, was deaf and could see very little, but she knew she had another child to train and so she held on for another 3 years. She finally passed away at the venerable age of 41, always a Princess and always living life on her own terms.

Darn if I don't miss the little gal, except possibly at vaccination time.

Chapter 8

Peaches, Cream and Reality

Trust in God, but tie your horse.

Anonymous

Owning horses is not always peaches and cream, I'm here to tell you. In fact, if I was a sane person, I'd have every right to absolutely hate a few of the four legged beasts.

"No, DON'T CUT OFF MY CUSTOM BOOTS!" I remember admonishing the folks trying to help me after my accident.

"Are my horse and saddle okay?" was the first question out of my mouth.

So, what happened? Well, on this lovely Fall morning I was involved in an eventing clinic. I cannot remember the clinician now. We had completed our dressage and stadium work, and we were now schooling the cross-country jumps. Really, I should have opted out, as I knew my horse could come unglued in the field. He was a show hunter, and never would have made an eventer, but he was what I had and I wanted to take this clinic.

"Darlene," said the clinician, "you're up next!"

My stomach did that typical little lurch, mostly in anticipation of starting. I just loved nearly any horse experience, and was not yet wise enough to know that you get your best success with a horse by finding what they do well. For example, a large, heavy Percheron would likely not be the ideal dressage horse, and it would be nearly impossible for a Tennessee Walker to compete as a Grand Prix jumper. The horse must be capable, mentally and physically, to do the job you choose for him.

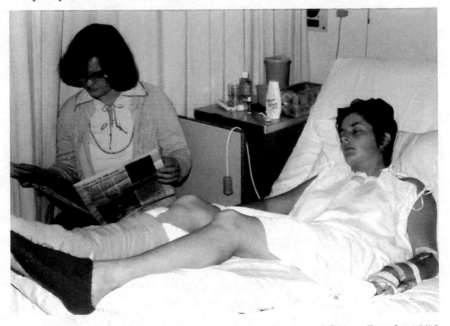

– Darlene and Sister Linda 1979

In my case, this 4 year old half thoroughbred/half appaloosa was spooky, unpredictable, and really not very well started. I had purchased him from an amateur woman who tried to train him herself. She figured that if he bucked and acted badly when she was riding, well, that meant he was in a" bad mood". So she would dismount, bring him back to the barn and feed him. If you have figured out that this horse behaved like a petulant child, you would be correct.

It didn't take long until the amateur woman who owned him had taught him that bad behavior meant that he could go back to the barn and eat, no matter what the hour of the day. Eventually, Buddy (ha!) was for sale. Being young and ambitious, and having little money, I decided to buy Buddy from the woman. His price was very inexpensive, largely because of his bad behavior. I just figured that with the right attitude adjustments, Buddy could be rehabilitated. He was jet black, with very small darker black spots on his rump. He moved very well, and was quite an athletic jumper. The quality was there in the exterior package, but the mind had been sadly corrupted. I really didn't hold the horse accountable for that.

So began my relationship with Dr. Buddy and Mr. Hyde! I referred to him as the horse with two personalities. He had an evil twin that would randomly show up, and when the evil one was there, all hell broke loose. By way of example, I can relate taking him to a horse show where he won three classes, all blue ribbons. Waiting for the fourth class, I was congratulating him and myself for a job well done. When my class was called, he and I calmly walked into the ring…same ring, same horses, same everything, just one hour later.

"Trot," came the command from the announcer. Buddy began with his beautiful trot, toes pointed, great movement from the shoulder, smooth, so smooth. "Canter," the announcer said, and then…the evil twin showed up! Buddy leaped into the air like he was shot out of a cannon. Hitting the ground, he arched his back up, doing the best bronc imitation he could muster. Then he bucked so hard his tail hit my hardhat! Picture this in your mind…watching it would have been awesome. He was very athletic. Riding on the back of this demon who had somehow replaced my previous horse, now that was crazy.

"One more of these bucks and I'm gonna be launched," I thought. So did the announcer. "Halt, all halt," called a very excited announcer. The other horses were beginning to react to my horse's bad behavior. (I should mention here that horses are herd animals, and will often "catch" hysteria from each other. As my horse was obviously in hysteria mode by now, I'm sure the announcer was trying to avert disaster.) I was doing my best not to crash into anyone, but really had my hands full just staying on.

Everyone in the ring came to a full stop, and when this happened, Buddy stopped too. Yes, there is a God! At this point, the announcer said, "You may be excused from the ring," at which point I gratefully left! Here was the winner of three classes previously, and we couldn't even finish the fourth one! In a nutshell, that was the story of Buddy's life. He had tremendous inconsistencies, and you could not tell when this would happen. No amount of preparation guaranteed sanity. His bad behavior had no consistent trigger that I could find. Wind, noise, and location seemed to matter little to him. I always was very consistent with his exercise, as I felt that too many days off for any equine was a sure way to guarantee excess energy. Every horseman or woman knows that you must be consistent in everything you do with horses, so that they know what to expect. I **never** took him back to the barn after bad behavior. I **never** failed to discipline him with a sharp word or a tap from my stick, if he deserved it. And I **never** failed to reward him with a kind word and a pat on the neck for good behavior, which he could deliver on many occasions.

> *You must be consistent in everything you do with horses*

Another situation comes to mind. It was a cold day in February, and the ground in my riding ring was frozen. Deciding to go out for a walk down the local country roads, I tacked up, pulled on my gloves and mounted. Although it was cold, the countryside was beautiful. The bare trees rose up in stark contrast to the overcast sky. The peacefulness of the day, the muted clip-clop of Buddy's hooves on the dirt roads lulled me into quiet introspection. Buddy ambled on, allowing me to have some "think" time, which I was enjoying. On and on we rode, putting some miles between us and the barn. It didn't seem to matter, as we had several hours of daylight for our return trip.

Suddenly, out of nowhere it seemed, a very cold wind came up. The sky turned from overcast to ominous. Buddy's ears perked up, as did his walk. "On no!" I thought. "Don't go ballistic now, Buddy!" That was not his intention that day. Horses are more tuned in to changing weather than humans are. Being tuned into weather changes could mean life or death for a horse in the wild. Although Buddy was a far cry from living in a "wild" setting, he still retained those instincts passed down in the DNA of thousands of years of equine existence.

I turned for home, which seemed like the prudent thing to do. Within a few minutes, ice pellets began to fall from the sky. With the increasing wind, these pellets hurt when they hit the exposed skin of my face. Buddy put his head down, trying to avoid the stinging ice. As the ice hit my eyelashes, it semi-melted there, freezing my lashes together! With cold fingers, I had to keep pulling my lashes apart, so I could see where we were going. My layers of clothing, comfortable when we started out, were now woefully inadequate. I could feel my core temperature dropping, in direct proportion to the increasing wind and ice storm.

Most horses have an uncanny ability to return to their barns.

This event occurred before the invention of cell phones, so I really couldn't call for help. The area was quite remote, so there wasn't even a barn in which to shelter. We just kept heading for home. It occurred to me that I was becoming disoriented, as snow replaced ice and everything turned into swirling whiteness. "Buddy, "I said, "now is the time I must trust you. Take us home!"

Most horses have an uncanny ability to return to their barns. Their sense of direction far exceeds human ability, and I was counting on this. By now, I couldn't feel toes or fingers, and hypothermia seemed a distinct possibility. On we trudged, heads down into the wind. What had started out as a lovely adventure now became something much more serious… for horse and rider. The ride that was intended to take only a few hours, now took much longer. Roads became slippery, and the road back seemed longer and longer.

Finally, through the snow and ice storm, I saw our house and barn in the distance. Buddy did bring us home. On his best behavior, in the most trying of circumstances, he rose to the occasion, and I was sincerely grateful! I want to be fair in telling Buddy's story, for every being has good in them. This was part of his "good".

So, back to the clinic. "Darlene, you're up!" Called the clinician. The task was to work through several cross-country jumps, which were designed to test the athleticism and obedience of horse and rider. I was excited! Several log jumps of about three feet high were on the course, along a fence line. Then came a small ditch to jump over, followed by a gate which took us into another field. We were getting along pretty well. The next obstacle was called a "sheep pen". Built in the side of the hill, it was a square of board fence, four-sided. We were to jump into the uphill panel, bounce in the middle, and jump out the downhill panel. So, the difficulty was that these two jumping efforts had very little space in between, and were going downhill. The sequence seemed difficult but doable to me, as I headed toward it. We took off well, jumped in, bounced, jumped out and then all hell broke loose! Buddy, heading downhill, had the advantage. Again, I felt his tail touch my helmet as he bucked hard. Then he added a back cracking body whip to the side. You've seen these in the rodeo, where the horse or steer bucks and whips his back end sideways. I'm told that I stuck with him for three of these tremendous bucks, but the forth got me. The saddle had become displaced by these bucking efforts, and when the saddle turned to the right, I was thrown into the air!

Now, I have hit the ground before that incident, and certainly afterwards as well, mostly regarding these falls as non-events, and part of the sport. But I remember flying through the air this time, tumbling forward and literally coming to rest on my feet! Don't know how I did it, probably a result of the extreme momentum. Ordinarily, landing on your feet is a good thing. However, I landed in a dry creek bed, downhill and to the right of the pen jump.

"Crack!!!" The sound of a gun going off startled me. "Great," I thought. "Not only have I been thrown from my horse, but now I've been shot!" The crack was so loud, that the spectators would later tell me that they heard it. I dropped to the ground from my standing position in the creek bed. It took me a few seconds to realize that I was not shot; the sound was my ankle shattering! I tried to stand again, and collapsed onto the round river rocks lining the area. People rushed in to help me. Beyond their shoulders I saw Buddy, saddle under his belly, running like crazy through the field.

"Please," I cried. "Someone catch my horse before he hurts himself. And my saddle, my new saddle, he's going to destroy it!"

Several people broke away from the rescuers and went to aid the horse. Someone helped me to lie down, as others began to assess the situation. "She's broken her leg," a man named Ray announced. It was pretty clear that something was very wrong, both from the sound of the injury when it happened, and by my agony, which had set in once the adrenalin of the fall left. "Let's take her boot off before her foot swells!"

A tall riding boot can serve as a splint for a broken limb

Immediately, he was trying to pull my boot off. I didn't scream, although I would have liked to. Trying to stay calm, I said "No, do NOT pull on my leg!" "Right, right," Ray said, "Let's cut it off!" Me again. "NOOOOO, don't cut off my custom boots! (The horse folks reading this know what custom made boots cost, but for others, let's just say I could see a thousand dollars or so flushing down the toilet.) "Nope, we have to get the boot off!" he said and began cutting. Now, I want to add here, for future reference if you are ever unlucky enough to be in similar circumstances, a tall riding boot can serve as a splint for a broken limb until you are able to get to a hospital. Ray didn't know about this, and was really trying to minimize my suffering, so cut he did.

This accident occurred in the middle of a field, on the side of a hill, and in a dry creek bed, so getting me out of there was going to be challenging. The owner of the farm hooked up a tractor and a hay wagon and came down to the creek. Several people lifted me into the bed of the hay wagon. Ray insisted on sitting in the wagon with me and holding my leg. People had gathered all around, including some young children, there with their parents. Tears were squeezing out of my eyes. One of the children asked if I would be okay. Something told me not to say "This hurts like hell!" Instead, I managed to say something lame like "oh, it's not too bad…"I really didn't want to sound or look discouraging to these young, potential riders, but I doubt that I fooled them.

Every jarring foot of that uphill wagon ride made me want to scream. Any movement was excruciating. Finally at the top of the hill, my sister waited with her car, and with me in the back seat (no Ray, thank God, as his well-intended helping was killing me), we proceeded to the hospital. After the usual wait in the lobby of the emergency room, I saw a doctor, who recommended an x-ray. By now, my foot was blue, and my ankle went one direction, and my toes another. Surely this foot is broken, I thought.

The skin could no longer contain the swelling

When the doctor returned, he pronounced the x-rays showed there was nothing broken, and that my ankle was badly sprained. I was to take pain medication, ice my foot and rest for three days, use crutches, and then try to walk, as comfort would allow. This seemed a little strange to me, as the color of my foot was growing increasingly blue and purple, and the pain was relentless, but until now I had never sustained a severe injury. I opted to trust the Doc.

Going home, I laid on the couch for a couple of days, with ice on the foot. By the third day, I needed to get a few things from the store for a trip I was to make to Richmond. I had been previously scheduled to deliver a lecture to a group in Richmond, which would require driving to the location and spending the night. I felt that I needed to get up off the couch and get moving!

Trying to shop at Wal Mart for toiletries was a disaster. I was sweating bullets from the pain, and, even though I was using crutches, my foot throbbed so bad I felt nauseated. My sister, Linda, said, "Come on. We are going to my doctor. This is not normal for a sprained ankle!"

Right she was! Dr. Weidig re-examined my injury and pronounced, "Young woman! You should not fool around with an injury like this! You could lose your foot!"

"What?" I replied. "You can lose a foot from a sprain?"

By now, my "sprained" ankle had swelled to three times its normal size. The skin could no longer contain the swelling, so fracture blisters had appeared, places where the skin had stretched and torn open from the pressure of the swelling. My foot was now blackish purple in color. I was indeed in trouble. Dr. Weidig sent me immediately to an orthopedist's office, for a consult. They took me right away.

When Dr. Chappell looked at my injury, he immediately ordered a new batch of radiographs. Trying to crutch down the hall to the x-ray lab, I wavered on my crutches. My face was ashen and sweaty. The x-ray technician, Mrs. Sipes, kindly said, "Let me get a wheelchair for you." "Oh no, I don't need a wheelchair," I replied, just as I went down for the count. Mrs. Sipes caught me, held me up by the loops on my jeans, and called for a chair.

The next few days were filled with disbelief, pain and medication for me. It turns out that I had fractured my talus bone, a bone that acts as support for the ankle. Not only was it broken, but one end of it was rotated away from the corresponding structure on my leg. Surgery had to be postponed until I could complete a round of very strong antibiotics for the infection that was setting in. Skin grafts were a distinct possibility, because of the extreme swelling. And the bone itself would need to be shaved, smoothed and fixated with metal pins. Everyday lost since the injury first occurred increased the chance the ends of the bone would reject each other. I don't know why or how the hospital missed seeing the injury and the break. Remember, they told me I had a sprain!

Well, to cut to the chase, I was admitted to the hospital for surgery one week and one day from the time of my injury. Entering the surgical suite, with plenty of medication in my system, the doctors later told me that I said, "Team work guys! Remember, two feet going in and two feet coming out. You do NOT have my permission to remove my foot!"

Today, I still have two feet, although I have had several surgeries since then to remove debris from the site. I did not walk unaided for a year after this injury, first in a wheelchair, then crutches and finally a cane. Even now, after a long day, I limp a little. One leg is shorter than the other because of the pinning and fusing of my talus bone. During my recuperative time, I would have someone help me onto the back of a trusted pony, Ginger, and I would ride her, cast and all. Some would think this foolish, but for me it was necessary for maintaining my sanity. I needed my horse fix, cast or no cast. Only a week after my cast was removed, I rode a horse (not Buddy) in a show at the Barracks in Charlottesville. And I got a ribbon! (Also good for my sanity, after being sidelined for so long.)

Speaking of sanity, I remember a strange incident that occurred while I was recuperating. In physical therapy, I was still using a cane 10 months after the accident. I strongly felt the accident had stolen a year of my life, and I had major concerns about the functionality of my ankle.

Out in the yard, my sister began to scream. "A snake! A snake!" She yelled. I hobbled out to see if she was in danger.

All horses are not suited for all things

"It's only a garter snake," I responded. "He's more scared of you than you are of him."

"Get rid of him!" Linda yelled again, still freaking out. (Guess you can tell that she has a thing about snakes?)

Normally, I would have just moved the snake to a less offensive spot, using a garden tool to lift him. But this day, pent-up rage and frustration burst forth. I began to flail away at the poor snake, hitting him repeatedly with my cane. This must have been some weird picture! Here is a woman beating a snake with a cane! The unfortunate snake bore the brunt of my anger, and soon he was definitely dead. I still feel a little bad about that.

You know, sometimes weird things happen for a reason. I learned that all horses are not suited for all things. Buddy went on to become a pretty decent trail horse, but came unglued in pressure or show situations. I learned that being "stoic" and "uncomplaining" is not always the best way, thanks to my sister Linda. I learned that "getting a second opinion", can make a huge difference, thanks to Dr. Weidig, and the Hess Orthopedic Clinic to which he referred me.

Further, I learned that you can meet wonderful people in the worst of times, as this is how I came to know Susan Sipes, the radiographic technologist who helped me that fateful day in the

— Darlene and Prince William

clinic. Her kindness to me during the various treatments helped me through a tough patch in my life, and she eventually became a great friend, the god-mother to my children and a companion in horse activities of various types. But that's another story...

Chapter 9

Prince William

For everything there is a season, and a time for every purpose under heaven.

Ecclesiastes 3: 1

I felt the need to go to the mountains this morning. And so I did, driving until the place felt right. At about 3, 500 feet, the trees are still bare, and the bite of winter is still in the air. Only the sun, warm on my back, reminds me of the coming spring. I pull over to a grove of pine trees, and sit down on a large, flat rock, trying to sort out my life.

C3&O

The year is 1979, and I am a young graduate student. I am also a rider recovering from a very severe horse riding accident. Thrown from the saddle over a downhill jump, my ankle shattered as I landed in a dry creek bed. It has been a long, hard, painful winter. In spite of the accident, the pins holding my ankle together, the ever present crutches and pain, I still want to ride. In fact, that need is part of the core of me. I believe it is written in my DNA, ancient and inborn. Still wearing a brace, unable yet to walk unaided, I know I need to get back in the saddle.

Sarah, my coach and friend, recommends to me a young three year old thoroughbred. "He is special, "she says. I think I am crazy to even look at a three year old thoroughbred cross, much less ride one. Considering that I haven't ridden in months, have only one good leg and the other leg is pinned together, the last thing I need is another accident. Reactive and sensitive by nature, young thoroughbreds are unpredictable. Even a "special" one could be a bad choice for me right now. Still, I go to look, mostly on the faith that Sarah knows a good horse when she sees one, and that she wants what is best for me.

Hobbling up on crutches to see this youngster, I am not disappointed. There he stands. Tall, bay and handsome for sure, Prince William is indeed quite appealing. His dark brown eyes are a curious mixture of youth and wisdom. Sometimes there are individuals that are just "born old", and despite their obvious chronological youth, they seem to have an understanding of the world beyond their years. He squirmed as I brushed him, shied when I led him from the barn, but he stood quietly as I mounted. Mounting gracefully was not possible for me right now, as my broken right ankle could barely support me long enough for my left foot to step into the stirrup. But somehow I got on, and we went on a little hack. His gaits were quite comfortable and smooth. Things were looking up, I thought, as I felt the warm promise of the March sun on my back. Perhaps this is a sign the harsh winter was over for me. Returning to the barn, I asked Sarah" Can I take him home and try him for a week? Then I'll know if he's the one."

Over the course of the next week, Willie and I had our highs and lows. He broke the crossties, the ropes suspended from the wall to hold an equine secure for grooming or saddling. He was green enough that any tension on his halter caused him to pull back and then SNAP! went the crossties and the halter. "This horse will cost me a fortune in leather and equipment at this rate." I thought. He pounded the stall wall every morning and evening, demanding his feed, an impatient guest at best. (He never gave up this method of opinionated eating, but that is getting ahead of the story.) A little flag of doubt raised in my mind, as halters and lumber could be expensive to replace.

However, impatience with grooming and eating was where his rude behavior ended. He was tolerant of my brokenness from the start, for it was more than just my leg that had been shattered. My world and my marriage had also come apart during the same year.

I won't say that Willie knew everything about women, marriages or broken bones, but I will say there was a natural kindness to his spirit that was indeed "special."

And he had a great heart. Horse people talk about "heart" in horses all the time, and it generally denotes an equine with uncommon drive and courage. Those who possess it will rise to the occasion, pulling ahead in the drive to the finish line, jumping large fences seemingly beyond the scope of their physical ability

There was a natural kindness to his spirit that was indeed "special".

or training, performing some fete with uncommon strength or determination. Or they will save your butt when you least expect it.

During the try-out week for Willie and me, we had occasion to go out for a field ride. The woods were quiet and the ground soft from a recent rain. As I cantered through the field, I felt a new hope and energy growing in me. Dodging trees and stumps, I spied a newly fallen tree, horizontally suspended two feet off the ground as it rested on its broken end. The approach was fairly clear and it seemed a good, natural obstacle. Willie, being very young, hadn't done much jumping yet, and I wasn't up to my usual level of riding due to my accident, but the little log seemed made to order and safe enough. It looked like a good start for both of us.

Pressing him forward, I did not notice the ground hog holes until the take-off stride. Ground hogs in Virginia never dig just one hole. They always have a front door and a back door, at the very least. Seeing these holes in the second of take-off for the jump, I knew I was in trouble. "This is where we die!" flashed through my head. "Sorry, Willie, it's all my fault." In my mind's eye, I could see Willie stepping into the holes, breaking his legs, and well, I couldn't even finish the thought.

The ground was soft and I felt both of his front feet sink deep into the holes at the base of the jump. Miraculously, this young horse rocked back onto his hocks, almost sitting down on the ground, sucked his front feet out of the holes and---unbelievably---jumped the log! Calmly landing on the other side, he cantered away across the field, clearly of the mind that it was all in a day's work.

I went back to the barn in awe of that young horse. He had great presence, tremendous heart and a new owner, me. I made arrangements to buy him that day. It was just meant to be. Sarah, knowing the my funds were extremely low due to my injury and being out of work, made the offer to let me pay $25 per month. Now, even in 1979, requiring such a small monthly payment was very generous. I think Sarah and Willie (the horse) were in cahoots to try and heal my leg and my life, and I decided to work with them.

Prince William was an exceptionally good mover

That was many years ago and there are many stories to tell about Prince William. He won nearly every flat class we ever entered. He was an exceptionally good mover, with an economy of movement and a ground-covering stride that most horse show judges appreciated. He was the Tri-State Pleasure Champion of Virginia, West-Virginia and Maryland at the age of four. By age six, he was a working hunter, jumping four foot obstacles with ease and confidence. Moreover, the boy could foxhunt too. He could be a bit of a spook if someone startled him, so I learned to sit tight. He could buck a little—ok, sometimes a lot—if the weather was cold or my attention level too casual. But time and again, he rose to each challenge with grace and courage.

Willie did have a few quirks. One was traveling. He never hauled well, kicking the trailer walls vigorously during transportation. The only thing that calmed him was music. We tried everything, rock, classical, contemporary, but this was a country music horse. The only thing that curtailed his trailer kicking was country music, specifically a group called *Alabama*. Any of their tunes were fine, but nothing else would do. So we got a tape player for his trailer, so he wouldn't destroy his hocks. Remember the old eight tracks? Well, I had every Alabama tape that had been made and I played them all for him. On one show day, I left the barn and, in my haste to pack bridles, saddles, helmet and buckets, I forgot the Alabama tapes. Improvising, I played others, The Beatles, the Rolling Stones, a little bluegrass…nothing worked. My trailer went bumping and thumping down the highway, with me praying the horse didn't injure himself in the process. It was a long ride…

Life went on, and we continued to show, local, the "A" shows, even Washington. Willie, excuse the pun, took all in stride. I still have more silver that he won for me than I have ever purchased for myself. Willie and I would have breaks in our show career as a new marriage, babies and a career had to be factored into our equation. I began to teach riding lessons during this period of time, and sometimes would let one of the students ride and compete on my "special" horse. He carried them as well, asking only that they give him direction and then stay out of his way. He knew the drill and did the job.

A real character in the field during turnout, he would often choose a pasture mate that he favored. Rajah the pony was one of those. Willie loved Rajah, and would herd him around the field, always keeping the pony close. Willie certainly found this closeness more charming than Rajah did. Finally this one-sided companionship came to a head, and Rajah jumped the four board fence, in an effort to evade the bossy Willie.

Without hesitation, Willie jumped the fence as well, and both disappeared into the neighbor's field. Before I could do anything about this development, here came Rajah back over the fence with Willie right behind him. Landing with grace on our side of the fence, Willie looked at me with the calm assurance that all was now in order.

As time marched on, the years of showing, trailering and wall-kicking began to take its toll on Willie's hocks. His working hunter career got scaled back a bit, lower jumps being easier on his body. Still an attractive fellow, dark bay, shiny, healthy, he could carry my students around a 2 foot or 2 foot 6 inch course in a competitive way. Willie was now 16 years old and a family member. I had promised him years ago that he would have a retirement plan if and when he needed it. Even when times were lean, and there were some of those times, I told him that if I had a home he did too. He was the only equine that I bought at age three and kept forever. He was with us through his twenties and then on to age thirty, when he did whatever he pleased. Eating, resting, sometimes playing in the field with his buddies, these were now his daily pursuits. He lived in a big paddock, and his view included mountains in every direction.

– Prince William 1980

Other horses and ponies came and went, good, honest, talented equines, with stories of their own. But Willie was indeed "special" and stayed in my barn and in my heart.

On March 29, 2006, he was cavorting with the other guys in his paddock at 5 p. m., and then was brought in for dinner. By 7 p. m., as I am teaching a student in the ring, I hear an unusual amount of banging in Willie's stall. Curious, I think, because he has already eaten, which is the usual stall-thumping time. I excuse myself from my student and go to check on him. He is standing in his stall, spraddle-legged, with a confused look in his eye. He then tries to walk around the 12 foot by 12 foot stall, banging into the walls. I slip his halter on, and carefully lead him from his stall. His legs barely support his body, buckling slightly from the effort.

Horses know instinctively that a down horse is vulnerable to predators

Trying to calm him, I yell for help. "Brooke, call the vet. Willie's in trouble!" The lack of coordination is unsettling to him. Brooke brings me some banamine, a pain and anti-inflammatory medication, which we administer in an effort to control his discomfort. I suspect some kind of cardiac event, which would not be surprising in a thirty year old horse. Still, I can't really imagine life without Willie around. He has been a part of my passage from youth to adulthood. He is as constant to me as the passing of the years. And now he is in trouble, big trouble. The vet is called, but cannot come immediately due to other calls ahead of ours.

As the minutes tick on, Willie struggles with balance and breathing. He is reluctant to lie down, although he seems exhausted and I wish he would rest. I am sure the instinct to survive, to stay on his feet, to keep on living drove him on. Horses know instinctively that a down horse is vulnerable to predators and they will try to stay on their feet if at all possible. Secretly and selfishly I hope that his great heart can sustain him. Finally he sinks to the ground, weak from his efforts to stand. As I kneel beside him, his breathing becomes so shallow that I think he is gone. The hour is now 9 p. m., and just as I start to say good bye to this faithful friend, he draws a mighty breath and heaves himself back to his feet. I tell him that this effort is impressive but unnecessary. I already know what a strong will he has.

My daughter Diana and I take him into our riding ring and turn him loose. He walks haltingly, trying to graze, nibbling a few bites of grass, trying to get back to his normal self. But he is weak, and goes down again. The process is repeated over and over, heartbreakingly, until finally, he lies still. I cover him with a blanket, and slip inside for a quick cup of coffee, my feet numb with the cold. Barely gone five minutes, I return to find him at the gate looking toward the house, waiting for me. He falls to the ground once again, and I sit beside him. "Stay down, Willie boy," I whisper. "Stay down. Your work is done. And I'll stay right here beside you."

"Where is the vet," I wonder. For the most part, we have controlled his pain, and his anxiety seems to have been relieved by the medications which I have given him. Still, I do not wish for him to suffer, and I want him to leave this life with the same dignity as he has lived it.

Since it is clear to us now that Willie is dying, Diana offers to bring Topper, her retired show pony and Willie's current best friend, into the ring to say good-bye. People often do not realize how powerful can be the link between equine friends. These two had become inseparable over the years. Topper, now nearly blind, had come to rely on Willie for security and protection from the other horses. They had their own routine. Every morning Willie would wait for Topper at the gate, and walk him out to the field. Stopping every few feet, he would call to the old pony, guiding him along. No other horses in the field were allowed to bother Topper. Willie was his guardian and protector. Every evening, Willie would find Topper, searching the field for him, as he sometimes wandered off on his own. Bringing him back up to the gate, they would wait to be led in for supper.

Diana brings Topper into the ring. Willie, lying flat on his side, opened his eyes and looked carefully at Topper, his pony buddy. Unbelievably, the old man hauled himself to his feet one last time. Unsteadily he made his way over to the blind pony, rubbing noses with him, breathing in the scent of his friend, touching him gently with his nose. Across the fence, a big grey horse stood watching the events. Willie looked up, seemingly bothered by the watcher. Carefully, painfully, he made his way over to the fence and stomped his foot as hard as he was able. Then, squealing, he pawed at the grey horse on the other side of the fence, putting on a show of dominance and protection for his old pony friend. The grey, startled by the vehemence of Willie's reaction to his presence, turned and galloped away. Then and only then did he make his way back to Topper, touching him once again. The message was clear. He, Willie, had chased away the enemies, as usual, and now Topper was safe.

His courage, dignity and heart had been an example to me

The effort of this final self-imposed duty was taking its toll. Incredibly weary now, Willie sank to the ground, still in control, still aware. Diana and I could barely contain our tears, as we witnessed the evidence of the love between these two equines. We had been joined in our vigil by Brooke, my other daughter. Shortly thereafter, the vet arrived. A brief exam told her what we already suspected: Willie's great heart could do no more. With my permission, the vet gave him medication to ease his passing, and I rubbed his muzzle until there was no more breath in him.

How amazing and startling it is to watch a life end. It is so very permanent. Thirty years of memories of life with Willie run rampant through my head, and I am almost dizzy with the impact of his passing.

With Brooke's help, I covered him with his horse blanket for the last time.

His courage, dignity and heart had been an example to me, even in death, and he is buried on our farm, next to the riding ring on the hill. Often, I look out my window and think of our escapades and I smile.

I am sad because my friend is gone, and with him my youth. He was a present I gave to myself in a transitional time of my life. With him I knew the adrenalin rush of the show ring, exciting runs in the hunt field and quiet hacks through the grassy fields. I am thankful to have had such a wonderful equine friend and partner. I could write volumes on how it felt to sit on his back, feeling his power under me. I loved the shows, the classes, the thrills. Every ride was a great adventure and all the more fun because of Willie's willing and able participation.

It has been 30 years since I first met Prince William. Surely he has lived up to his name, and surely he was "special".

CH80

So, I drove to the mountain once again, Willie's passing on my heart. I had come here before, to dream of owning a horse who would restore my joy in life and give me a renewed sense of wellness. Now I came to sit on this rock and deal with my grief at his loss. It is no comfort that I own 20 other horses, and have had countless rides on many other equines. Willie was still personal and "special" to me.

A big black crow has landed on the branch above my head, taunting the other birds around him. "Caw, caw, caw, "he calls out. Is there a message here? It seems the crow is talking to me. Life goes on, he seems to say, and these things are all in the normal course of events.

Winter gives way to Spring and the March sun is once again warm on my back. And me, well I'm sitting here on this flat rock, warmed by the sun. It is the perfect place to tell Willie's story.

Chapter 10

The Gifts

"You are not working on your horse, you are working on yourself."

Ray Hunt

From time to time, I am asked to do field trips for different or-ganizations. I have had pre-schools come to visit, sponsored a field day for asthmatic children so they could learn to enjoy farm settings and still be safe within their pulmonary boundaries. I have had colleges visit and judging teams of 4-H youth come to practice by evaluating my horses. Special needs groups have come for tours and pony rides. But by far the most moving experience, for me, was a visit by the local pre-school special needs program.

On this occasion, a group of 19 children came to visit. They were 3 and 4 year olds, with a variety of special needs represented. Some of these children were visually impaired, others had learning disorders. Some had difficulties with hearing, or with understanding what they were hearing, while others had behavioral issues. But our focus was not on limitations, but on enabling. We wanted the children to experience the unique connections that can be made between horses and humans.

In preparation, my barn folks had helped me set up several areas of interest, including a grooming area, a get-your-picture-taken-if-you-want-to area, and a pony ride area. Dividing the groups up, 6 children groomed, while 6 rode, etc.

I obviously chose the horses carefully. I could not use a horse that was sensitive to loud noises, as some of the children would spontaneously burst out with loud vocalizations. I needed quiet, calm horses that would accept unusual movements and noises and energy, and not become alarmed.

In the grooming area, I chose to use Merlin, a very large grey Percheron, who belonged to Edith, one of my students. Merlin was a massive fellow, but for all his giant size, his heart was pure gold, and his temperament was stellar. He would stand for hours to be groomed and brushed. In short, Merlin was perfect for this job.

In the ring, we had Penny, a little quarterhorse mare. In lessons she was capable of performing at the walk, trot and canter, and could be motivated into jumping if someone insisted, but she really preferred this sort of day. So Penny would give these little children pony rides safely.

A second equine for the riding part of this outing was Blaze, a little bay quarterhorse that I acquired from Dr. Don Cromer, when the Therapeutic Riding Program at his farm was discontinued. So Blaze was a shoe-in, having worked with special needs children before.

As the children arrived, we organized them and their teachers and helpers into groups, sending them to the various interest centers already described. In the riding area, the teacher would bring me one of the children, tell me his or her name, and I would walk around the riding ring slowly, talking softly and cheerfully to each one. I had Blaze, and another handler was walking Penny. Some of the children required side-walkers to keep them from sliding off the saddle. As I walked these little folks around, most would look very pleased to be sitting up high on the back of the horse. Some squealed in delight, a few rocked back and forth on the saddle, still others smiled silently and did not utter a sound.

At the end of the trip around the ring, the teacher would take the picture of each student on the horse, to be used in the classroom and eventually to send home to mom and dad. I felt proud to be able to offer this experience to these children. Little did I know, however, that I was about to receive a far greater gift the one I gave.

After we had been giving the rides for a little while, the teacher sat a small little boy onto Blaze's saddle. "This is Jonas," she said. And off we went, Jonas, Blaze and I. As we walked, I made conversation with the little guy. "Have you ever ridden before?" No answer. "Do you like horses?" No answer. "I'm really glad you could visit today, Jonas." Still no response from him, but I could tell by his look of pure absorption that Jonas was enjoying his ride. As we drew closer to the teacher waiting to bring me the next rider, Jonas said in a loud, raspy voice, "RIDE MORE!"

I smiled and the teacher, surprisingly, began to cry. Tears dripped from between her lashes as she said, "Those are the first words he has ever spoken. Could you please take him around again?"

Horses do not like to have their legs trapped

"Of course," I said quietly, almost afraid to say anything to break the spell. I guess I should admit that I got a little misty too, it was just such a tremendous event for all of us. His FIRST words! And I had the honor of hearing them. Blaze had the honor of being the catalyst, the tipping point, the fulcrum between a world of silence and a world of communication for this little child. We could only hope that those words would be the first of many.

When Jonas left the riding station, he went over to big, old Merlin, all 1600 pounds of him, standing in the grooming area. Before anyone could intervene, Jonas attached himself to one of Merlin's giant hind legs. By attached, I mean *attached, wrapped around and hugging tightly!* Everyone present collectively caught their breath, afraid to move and startle Merlin, or cause him to step on the little boy. Merlin, however, seemed to sense that Jonas meant him no harm, and indeed *needed* to be wrapped around his leg.

At this juncture I need to mention the natural instincts of horses everywhere, which are to react as prey animals. That means, for one thing, horses do not like to have their legs trapped by anything, because being trapped and unable to move your legs freely can lead to being hunted by a predator. Now of course little Jonas was not much of a predator, but to a horse it is difficult to sort out who is allowed to trap your legs and who is not allowed to do so.

So all the adult horse people present were afraid for Jonas, and wanted to peel him off Merlin's leg. But Merlin turned his big head, smelled deeply of the little boys scent, and then went back to dozing while the other children brushed him. Jonas clung there for a full five minutes or more, deeply absorbed in his own experience of Merlin. What was Jonas thinking? What was he noticing about Merlin? Had the interaction with the horses unlocked the shell that he lived in? I don't know, really.

If I close my eyes, I can try to imagine Jonas' experience. I can imagine the smell of the horse, unique and of nature. I can imagine feeling his breathing going in and out, moving my body slightly as I clung to his leg. His leg would be fuzzy and warm against my cheek. Would I feel Merlin shift his weight to the other leg, as horses often do? Was Jonas feeling anxiety or peace? Were all of these feelings stimulating Jonas on a conscious level or as a tidal wave of sensory input?

We will never know for sure. But Jonas gave me the gift of his first words, and his teacher promised to talk to Jonas' parents regarding more horse experiences and opportunities for this child. I hope the parents followed up somewhere and used more horse experiences to open Jonas' communication channels.

Again, I had experienced the primal connection between equine and human, a connection almost inborn and a little difficult to explain. You almost have to experience it. You almost have to see it. And Blaze, Merlin and I had provided Jonas his opportunity to "connect" and leave his silent world, if only for a short time.

◦◦◦

Billy was a student sent to me by his pediatrician. At age 10, he had sustained a severe brain injury in a car crash. After the physical healing, it became obvious there was damage to the part of his brain which controlled emotion, decision-making, and concentration. As Billy had a fascination with horses, his doctor and his mom sent him to me. The hope was that his interest in horses would encourage him to concentrate better, and learning to ride would retrain the brain and strengthen organizational skills.

Billy was indeed passionate about horses! And he was also brilliant. The accident had not changed his innate intelligence. But his manipulation of information was different. Every word I said, he memorized. He was very literal in his acceptance of information. If I explained something on Monday, and then mentioned it in a different way on Friday, his mind saw that as error. He was not able to understand that "posting trot" and "rising trot" could be thought of as the same thing. You can see how this could make teaching a bit of a challenge. Still I enjoyed working with Billy. I could see improvements, slow at first, but I loved his enthusiasm.

Eventually, he mastered the basics, and moved on to jumping small jumps. This took a year or so, but he persevered. He would ask questions like, "Does the horse *know* he's a horse?" (Try answering that one!) And "Why do you call this horse grey when he is really white?"

About two years into our riding experience, Billy really wanted to go to a show at a local barn. We had been practicing riding easy courses at home. Low jumps were not a problem, but memorizing the courses (the order in which the jumps would occur) was a big issue.

While Billy could describe in detail the colors and shapes of the jumps, he struggled with remembering which jump should be first, second, third, etc. And, in a show, the order was important. Much to Billy's credit, he wanted to try and tackle this new challenge.

We went to a show at a nearby facility, and we were as prepared as we could be. The horse, Jaz, was clean and shiny, and just about as bomb-proof as a horse can be. Extremely cooperative and very competent over fences, I trusted her to do whatever Billy asked of her. She was one of my best school horses. But Billy would have to tell her which jump to go to and in which order. Could he do it? I wanted him to be successful, and not be frustrated or hurt if things did not go well.

While we were waiting for Billy's turn to go into the ring, we rehearsed the order of the jumps, looking at a posted diagram of the course. I went over and over the order, and then Billy repeated it back to me. Still he seemed to have some confusion about which direction to go and which jumps to do.

Billy seemed at peace with being here at the show, and with going into the ring alone to do his course of jumps. "I can do this, Darlene, "he declared. "And I really want to get a blue (first place) ribbon!"

I really appreciated the resolve I saw in this young boy's eyes. He was determined to follow his dream and was working hard to overcome the organizational deficits created by his accident. Not only was he willing to try this event, he wanted to WIN it! I should mention here that Billy's class had 22 entries in it, meaning that he was competing against 21 other riders, of all varying levels of expertise and training. *I* was hoping he would jump all the jumps in correct order and not get hurt. *He* wanted to do those things, AND win the class.

At last his number was called, and into the ring they went. The start was a bit rough, as Billy began to go the wrong way. Realizing his error, he reversed direction and started again. He finished the course in good order, but would receive no ribbon since he started incorrectly.

> *Not only was he willing to try this event, he wanted to WIN it!*

"That's okay, Billy," I said. "You jumped around great, and you completed your course!"

Billy replied, "I want to do the second course, and I know I can remember it."

What a guy! So we began again, memorizing the second course. We looked at the diagram, we watched other riders take their turns, we discussed and repeated the course over and over. Finally, he said, "I'm ready. I can do it and I really want to get a blue ribbon."

"Ride your best, Billy, and everything will be all right. I know you can do it too!" In my mind, I was already saying a little prayer. This blue ribbon probably meant more to Billy than to anyone else there. It would mean that he could tackle the same challenges as other "normal" people. It would signal to his parents, watching from the spectator area, that their son was recovering, rebuilding brain skills wiped away by his accident. And it would say to me that I was helping him. Oh, how we all wanted that blue ribbon for him! But getting it was an extreme long shot.

Once again, Billy was called into the ring for his turn. He looked at me one last time, flashed me his big grin and then he started. This time, he began in the correct direction. Approaching jump one, his pace was wonderful. He and Jaz cantered down to fence one and fence two beautifully! Into the far corner of the ring they cantered, executed a perfect lead change, and continued to the second line of jumps. Eyes up and the picture of concentration, Billy guided Jaz to fences three and four, and then turned the corner. I prayed that he would choose the correct third line of jumps. He did! On his way to jumps five and six, I was almost trembling with excitement. His trip so far was really nice, but there were still two jumps remaining.

No matter what the judge says, you are truly a winner!

On he went, turning for the last two jumps. And they were awesome! "You did it, Billy! You did it!" I was jumping up and down as he came out of the gate, and the grin on his face said it all. "Did I win?" he asked.

"Billy," I replied, "No matter what the judge says, you are truly a winner! Your course was beautiful, you did everything right, and I am so proud of you!"

Billy's parents had come down from the spectator seating at this point to hug and congratulate their son. And while we were enjoying this moment, the show announcer began to call the placing's for the class. "And first place goes to …Billy M. riding Kemper Knoll's All That Jaz!"

Time stood still for a moment…We all looked at each other. Out of twenty-two riders and horses, Billy had WON the class! I had to look away for a moment, as a little tear rolled down my cheek. Billy's mom had a veritable flood coming from her eyes, and his dad was a little misty too. The only person that was calm and matter- of- course was Billy, who said "I just knew I could do it! And I got the blue ribbon!"

CB&O

On another occasion, a friend of mine asked if I would give her elderly mother a driving lesson with one of the farm's miniature horses. There were several complicating issues with this request.

The first problem is the mother was visiting on Sunday, and I had plans for Sunday morning. My schedule often keeps me very busy on weekends, as that is when most horse shows are scheduled. On this particular weekend, I had been at a horse show all day on Saturday, and really wanted to be "off" on Sunday. I had found a church that nourished my spiritual life, and I really tried to attend whenever I could, even if that meant somewhat sporadically. So I had plans to attend services at 1030 a. m. I offered to teach the mother in the afternoon. Unfortunately, it was going to be a hot day, and the potential student could not come in the heat of the day.

Which brings me to problem number two. The mother who wanted to take the lesson was 84 years old! Teaching someone in that age group requires courage and cooperation on the part of the teacher, the equine and the student! Did I really want to try this?

Somehow, I could hear in Anita's voice that this was a "special" request. "I don't get to see my Mom very often, and I really wanted to share this horse experience with her. She rode in her youth and throughout her middle years. It would mean so much to both of us. I know this is an imposition, but…"

"O.K. Anita," I responded. "Let's go for it! Ten o'clock on Sunday morning."

Sunday came, and it was a beautiful day. The sky was somewhat overcast, but it was still quite warm. Since it was mid-morning, the full heat of the day was a few hours away, so our timing was fortunate. Anita arrived with the cutest little lady, all 4 feet 11 inches of her! Her mother, Marta, is from Guatemala, and had a charming accent from that part of the world. She was dressed barn-appropriate and seemed eager to learn about the miniature horses and the sized-down carriages they pulled.

I spoke of the inauspicious beginnings of miniatures in this country, of their jobs as cart-pulling horses in the mines, often towing up heavy loads of coal from deep in the earth. I talked about the transition of these little animals from beasts of burden to pleasure animals. Their purpose at my farm was to give lessons to people learning how to put a horse to a cart and drive. The carts and carriages are uniquely balanced to offer the least amount of weight to be put onto the horses' backs. The harness is padded to provide maximum comfort as each of these tiny equines performed their duties. As far as the "cute" factor, these little horses have a distinct edge, and add to that their usually quiet natures and willing attitudes, and we have a recipe for some fun and learning.

A quiet but firm hand tells the horse about the rider's wishes

Marta seemed eager to get into the cart, so I finished "putting to" (harnessing), and drove the cart into the riding ring. After driving the horse around the ring for a trip or two, I stopped to pick up my special passenger. We would ride together in the cart, with Marta sitting beside me. In her wrinkled face, her eyes were bright. She was ready to do this, no doubt. She kept repeating that she never expected to have this opportunity. As I talked with her, it became very apparent that she was an experienced horsewoman, and she understood what I was talking about. I spoke of handling the reins, of the similarity of feel, whether driving or riding. The reins being connected to the bit in the horse's mouth, a quiet but firm hand tells the horse about the driver's or rider's wishes as to direction and speed. After 15 minutes or so, I thought maybe Marta was getting fatigued. No way! When I asked if she wanted to stop, her comment was, "Oh, please, no! Please go on!"

So on we went, but this time I offered to let her drive. "Do you think I can?" she inquired.

"Of course you can! I'll just ride along beside you in the seat." Almost tenderly, she took the reins. Secretly, I hoped that I was doing the right thing. I did not want to betray Anita's faith in me by letting anything happen to her Mother! But I knew the horse was trustworthy and Marta, although aged, was *a horsewoman.*

At first tentatively, and then with increasing confidence, Marta drove around and around the ring. Soon she was turning and going in the other direction. In her eyes I saw "the look", the look that said she was "back in the saddle", so to speak. The years melted away as she gave the horse signals for walk and trot and halt. She paused for a moment, and I suggested that I should get out of the cart and Anita, her daughter, ride with her. Anita started to protest, but then relented, obviously excited to have this experience with her Mother. Away they went. The driving lesson was now approaching an hour and a half! I never would have expected the 84-year-old to have the energy and ability to "hang in there" for that length of time. Another daughter and grandson had come along for the outing, and she offered them rides in the carriage, each one in turn riding beside her as she drove them around the arena.

Sometimes the event becomes almost a spiritual experience

Everyone seemed happy, each for their own reasons, and probably no one was happier than I. This was a tremendous example of horses bringing joy into our lives and erasing the age barrier, if only for a little while.

At the conclusion of the driving time, Marta and Anita helped me groom D. J., the mini that was pulling the cart. They were lavish in their praise for the little guy, brushing his silky mane and grooming his back and legs. They spoke of his obedience, the quality of his movement, the correctness of his conformation. The two ladies were definitely horsewomen.

Anita took me aside and asked the question I had begun to dread. "How much do I owe you for this lesson? I know we have been here a long time, and on Sunday!"

From the start, I had planned to charge for this lesson. It did take my time and energy. We did use my horse, cart and harness. I *am* in the lesson business, and *it is* what I do. But as the lesson had progressed, and as I saw the love in the eyes of Marta and Anita as they shared this time, I became increasingly aware that this was not *just* a driving lesson. I could not charge for this. It was an emotional experience for me. I became aware there is more than one way to recharge my spiritual engine…and there should be no money involved!

And so I replied, "No, Anita, no charge. You gave a gift to your Mom, and she gave a gift to me. There can be no charge. I was honored to have the opportunity to share this with her, to enjoy the love of horses with a kindred spirit. This was a gift for all of us."

I think Anita understood.

Throughout my lifetime with horses, there have been occasions where the experience was more than just the physical act of riding or driving horses. Sometimes the event becomes almost a spiritual experience, a connection between horse and human that I just wouldn't miss for anything…and certainly money had nothing to do with it.

Chapter 11

Just Step Back

To err is human. To forgive, equine.

Anonymous

It takes a certain kind of person to live on a farm. The common understanding is that here in the country we lead stress-free lives, in harmony with nature. We get up with the chickens, we go to sleep when the sun goes down, and the whole picture is one of bucolic bliss.

Ha! The rewards of this lifestyle are many, but the stresses are many too. We live at the whim of Mother Nature. A freak storm can ruin a crop ready for harvest, a broken belt on a tractor can interrupt hay baling just when you need to get the hay out of the field before an impending storm. And, while you may have gotten up with the chickens, if you have a sick or ailing animal you stay up way after the chickens go to bed.

An injury to farm animals can mean a big vet bill (when you can't fix it yourself), a rise in grain prices can mean cutting back on your livestock or finding some other way to cut back your expenses to make up the difference. An injury to one of us (the humans) can be catastrophic, because we do physical work every day. By now, you are getting the idea…

A farmer/agri-business person must be 1/4 gambler, 1/4 veterinarian, 1/4 animal husbandry specialist and 1/4 horticulturist.

It takes a lifetime to acquire these skills…and just about when you think you've got it, something happens to remind you that there is always more to learn!

— Whit and Darlene at home 2011

My husband is a grand mix of all of these things. The only time he has spent away from our farm is when he was in school at Virginia Tech. There he learned the "technical" aspects of agricultural engineering, and the rest he has acquired through hands-on experience since he was born. He learned about babies by watching the cows give birth. He learned about hard work by helping his father, George W. Kemper, III, to maintain the farm while he was also Clerk of the Court for Rockingham County, Virginia, for 20 years. You see, the love of the land runs strong in Whit's veins, passed down from his father, whose ancestors moved here in the late 1700's.

One of the first four families to settle in what is now East Rockingham County, the Kemper's came from a long agricultural tradition. However, there have been Kemper's who have been doctors. People often named their babies after the doctor who delivered them, hence there are people in this area (now in their late 80s and 90s) who have the first name of Kemper, after the Dr. Kemper who assisted in their birth sometime in the early 1900's. (As an aside, family lore has it that Dr. Kemper was desperate to curtail this practice of having babies named after him. So, he started telling his patients that it was bad luck to give babies his name, as they usually died if so named. This was, perhaps, a little drastic, but it seemed to work!) We have had several Kemper's who were lawyers, including Albert Strayer Kemper, who once owned Bogota, the family home place in Rockingham County. We have Kemper's who have been politicians, as with Whit's father, who was elected several times to the Clerk of the Court position. Nearly all of these men farmed part-time or were the overseers of their properties, and led full-time or part-time agricultural lives.

It is no surprise that my husband, Whit, has close links to the soil. Really, I don't think he could be happy anywhere else. He cares about his livestock, takes pride in producing good hay, looks out over the farm at the end of the day thinking about what he will do in the morning, when he starts again. This is romantic in a way, but it also means that he doesn't really enjoy traveling or vacationing. He feels that going to the beach would be just fine if he didn't have to put up with all that sand! Being away from home overnight is a chore rather than a relief. *It takes a special personality type to deal everyday with the problems of farm life*, but he does it.

For those who know Whit, this story will come as no surprise. For the rest of you, well, enjoy!

Every year, when our children were ages 8 to 18, our family would participate in the local agricultural Fair, where they would exhibit their best animals, including sheep, steers and pigs. This meant that we were all together as a family for a week, pulling together to get home chores done so that we could go to the Fair and participate in the various animal shows. More importantly, however, was the chance to take the products of our farm to "town" and spend time together grooming them, caring for them and each other. All summer, the kids and the parents would train these animals to walk and behave while being handled by humans. Feed programs would be established and re-established to get these animals to peak condition by Fair time. The animals would be exercised to develop muscling (no excess fat) and conditioning.

The Fair was a fun time for our family, but also a tiring time, especially for Whit, who spent hours shearing sheep, weighing them, feeding them, buying the feed that they needed to flourish, consulting with family friends (also farmers) as to which ones to exhibit and which ones would stay home. These chores were added on to his already-full days. He did this because the children loved it. He did this because they were proud of their farm heritage and life-style and he wanted to encourage them. It was always extra expense and extra time, both things which are often in short supply on a farm. Because he is a good father and a good farmer, he saw the positive aspects of all this effort and expense, and he supported them. I helped where I could, but mostly the Fair was a bonding experience between this man and his children…and I loved it!

There really is no substitute for spending time with your children.

There really is no substitute for spending time with your children. It creates bonding, memories and trust. In today's rapid-fire, instant gratification society, perhaps what is missing is the time set aside for family adventures. Family activities which involve each member doing what they do, contributing to the whole experience and spending time together, those times are character-building and family-building.

On one such Fair morning, Whit set off for town to water and feed the show livestock already on grounds at the Rockingham County Fair, while I stayed home to teach a few riding lessons. He had been gone about an hour when I got a phone call.

Me: *"Hi Whit. How are the animals?"*
Whit: *"Don't know yet."*
Me: *"Oh, really? Why?"*

Whit: "*Well, the truck is on fire...*" (This said in his usual quiet
  voice)
Me: "Did *you say that the truck is on fire?*) (Hysteria starting to
  build)
Whit: "*Yep. On fire. (Still quiet voice)*
Me: "*Whit! The truck's on fire!! !)* (Full-fledged hysterical by
  now) "*Are you hurt? What happened? What did you do?*"
Whit: "*I stepped back... and called 911.*" (Very matter-of-fact,
  very calm)

— A Rainbow over the Barn

As it turns out, the model of Ford F250 that we owned at the
time was prone to carburetor problems, and a buildup of gas in the
carburetor had provided too much fuel, which burst into flames.
Evidently, when this happened, Whit grabbed the fire extinguisher
that we kept in the cab of the truck and tried to put the fire out,
but it was instantly a bigger fire that could be controlled. So, in
characteristic fashion, he called 911 and "stepped back".

Never prone to exaggeration, Whit handles things as they
come, calmly, safely, without the hysteria which can overwhelm me
from time to time. I am, by nature, an energetic, get in and get it
done kind of person. But sometimes such events as these can "blow
my mind". Not him. And, as it turns out, Ford Motor Company
replaced motor, wires, *carburetor*, etc., and threw in a paint job. I

guess they were just grateful that no one got hurt in our truck fire…*and so was I.*

The human reaction to everyday experiences in rural life can be quite interesting, to say the least. I am prone to call everyday an adventure. One such adventure occurred when I was alone at the farm, and needed to give an antibiotic injection to a rather fractious horse. Since no one else was at home, I decided to hold this horse with one hand, and inject him with penicillin with the other. I have done the same many times, and really did not see a big problem with getting this chore done. The horse had injured itself, had required stitches in a front leg, and the antibiotics needed to be given on schedule to prevent any infection.

Filling the syringe with the penicillin, I then put the halter on the horse, holding him with the attached lead rope. As I went to inject him, this guy reared up, front feet flailing over my head. Well, I was determined NOT to let the horse get away, and I was also determined not to waste the syringe full of penicillin. The syringe had flown into the air from the horse rearing, and I tracked it with my eyes, hand reaching up to catch it.

Catch it I did! The syringe had been flung eight feet into the air, and so came down with a good deal of force, where it landed in my upstretched hand! Actually, I should say in my outstretched arm, for the syringe and NEEDLE plunged into the vein on the underside of my wrist, *discharging fully half of its contents into my vein!*

This was not a good development, as I had never taken any penicillin. My father almost died from a penicillin allergy, and so our family doctor had recommended that his children abstain from using that particular antibiotic. Quickly, I put the horse back into his stall. This event happened before cell phones, so I began to run toward my house, to call 911!

Running, blood spurting from my arm, heart pounding in my ears, I thought, "Running makes my blood pressure higher and makes this penicillin circulate faster. Go slow, go slow. Control your breathing. "Crap, I felt like I could hear the funeral bells ringing already!

Reaching the house, I sat next to the phone and dialed 911.

"Please connect me with the Poison Control Center! This is an emergency!" I shouted into the phone.

The voice on the other end responded with "What is the nature of your emergency?"

"I was giving a horse a shot of penicillin and the needle went into my arm and I am allergic, or I might be allergic, and I don't know how much of the horse dose of penicillin went into my arm, and my face is hot, and my arm is bleeding, and…"The words fell out of my mouth in a cascade of information.

It was obviously too much information for this 911 call receiver. "Let me get this straight, "she said. You were giving medicine to a *horse, but then you took it yourself?*" she queried?

> # Just let it fall. You can always get a new one

"*Look lady,*" I responded, "*I think time may be important here!* I didn't mean to take the medicine. It just happened. My family is allergic to penicillin, and I may be too. And I just had a horse-sized dose! Can you check with the doctor and tell me what to do?"

With what sounded suspiciously like a muffled guffaw, she put me on hold. *On hold!* The minutes of my life ticked by, and I wondered if I would soon enter into anaphylactic shock. I mourned for all the things I would never do because of my bad decision to catch a needle and syringe in mid-air. (Take it from me: Just let it fall. You can always get a new one.)

"Hello, hello," came the voice on the other end of the phone, my lifeline, my hope for survival. "Umm, the doctor wants to know how you feel right now."

"I am stressed, but still breathing, "I replied. "And nothing is swelling up yet."

"Just a moment, "replied the voice. I thought I heard that muffled sound again. Was it a *giggle? Was this medical professional laughing at my dire situation?* Surely NOT!

"Well," the voice continued, "The doctor says if you are not dead already, then you will probably be okay. Stay by the phone for the next few minutes, just in case…"

"What?" I exclaimed with some degree of aggravation. "That's it? Really?"

This time the giggle was not very well contained. "Sorry, but we have never heard of such a situation before. And…and, well, ah, the doctor also says that you probably won't need any other antibiotic for a few months…"

Strange, but true.

– Hope and Darlene

Chapter 12

For the Love of Hope

The word <u>Chivalry</u> is derived from the French <u>cheval</u>, a horse.
Thomas Bulfinch (1796-1867)

On a farm, there are actually five seasons. They are Spring, Summer, Fall, Winter and Mud. On this particular morning, we were coping with the ravages of Mud. Winter snow melt and subsequent rain had turned our normally serviceable paddocks into slip-and-slides. Tromping through the deep mud was both difficult and messy. I was worried about the frisky horses injuring themselves. Sheer, joyful good spirits can and have caused horses to injure themselves with playful bucking and running, which can lead to a bad fall if surface conditions are not good.

My horses had been kept in their stalls for a few days, waiting for the ground to dry a little. They were now most anxious to be set free to do what horses do—run and play. Usually I love to watch their graceful bodies flying around, tails flagged out behind them, neighing to each other, and looking like the very embodiment of energy. Today, I was worried.

Thanks for the Memories or Marcy (as we called her at the barn), a big warmblood mare, was being particularly fractious. She was a gorgeous sight, gleaming dark bay body rearing and bucking, playful and without a care. I, on the other hand, had lots to worry about. This mare was an open jumper competitor, regularly jumping obstacles in competition which are four feet high and five feet wide. Good, strong, sound legs and feet are essential for her job. A strain, a cut, a tendon injury, or worse, could be career ending. I just couldn't take the pressure so I decided to bring her back in after a very brief turn-out time.

Playing tag with someone roughly ten times your size.

Going to the gate, I grabbed her halter and lead rope, closed the gate behind me and whistled. Normally, she would trot right up and permit herself to be caught. She is not usually a foolish mare during turn-out, but today her pent-up energy was overruling her good judgment. She ran straight at me, gaining speed as she came. Then she whirled about, bucked and took off again. Several times we went through this drill: run, buck, whirl, repeat. Mud flew with every movement and the mare seemed to delight in this. Such a game might seem like fun to some, if you don't mind playing tag with someone roughly ten times your size. As you might imagine, the horse was definitely having more fun than I was.

Again she ran towards me, enjoying her own game. This time, however, she got a little bolder, gaining speed, coming straight at me. As she went to do the whirl maneuver, something went wrong. She started sliding, 1250 pounds of out-of-control horse. The mud flew, clods striking me in the face. She couldn't stop in time, and now we both knew it. She was going to hit me!

I tried to get out of the way, but my boots stuck in the mud. There was nothing else to do but cover my head, close my eyes and pray. I have always believed in the power of prayer, and I pray with frequency. At this moment, I prayed with *urgency!* I knew the chances for injury were great and it was my own fault for being in the wrong place at the wrong time. I heard a scream from one of the helpers at the barn, who was watching this situation from the other side of the gate.

The next second I felt impact, but it was not the bone crushing I was expecting. I was being pushed along through the mud, driven by a large body, but I was not in pain. Does it take a while for injury to register on a brain in shock? My brain registered pressure, but not actual pain…What had happened?

Skidding to a halt, I opened my eyes, and the horse body touching me was red! Somehow, another horse in the same field, a chestnut mare named Hope, has gotten her body between me and the bay mare, and had taken the hit for me! *How she got there so fast, how she knew to protect me, why she decided to intervene*, these things I'll never know. But she did it, risking injury to herself in the process. I'm sure the collision of those two horse bodies did not feel good to either of them, but the two equines were well-matched in size and better able to survive a collision than an equine and a person. Both were shaken, but okay; and I, thanks to the bravery of a horse named Hope, well, I lived to tell this story.

Hope was kind of an interesting girl from the start. I found her on the recommendation of another horse professional, who knew her current owner was less than happy with her. Trying her out, I immediately liked her, despite the admonition that "she is kind-of a bitch." You know the old saying: one woman's trash is another woman's treasure. I rarely take a single opinion as definitive.

In our first ride, I found her willing enough, although she seemed a little high-strung and nervous. In the equine community, some horses are nervous types, others are quiet, some are rowdy and still others are placid. Their emotional make up runs the complete gamut of choices, much as the human species sees great variety in personality types. The "trick" is in matching up the horse's personality with a rider of complementary temperament. Some good equestrians can ride a variety of horse types, but even they will tell you they prefer a particular type of "ride". Every experienced rider knows the type of horse that suits them best, and that is what they call their "ride".

Was Hope my "ride"? I didn't know that for sure, but I instinctively liked her. So, I took her home. Early on, it was obvious that she wanted to know what was going on at all times. Fast movements made her break things, like cross-ties, ropes and halters. Loud noises also set her off. She was not the ride for someone inexperienced or easily intimidated. She wanted consistency, routine, balance. And she could read minds! Well, okay, maybe it just seemed like it, but she reacted to subtle body position adjustments when you rode her. If you sat still, she was quiet. If you were in an angry mood (even if it had nothing to do with her), and fiddled with the reins, or slapped the saddle onto her back, or rode with inconsistent aids, she became anxious and worried.

> *Without understanding, the mare became sullen and difficult.*

It turns out that her previous owner had been trying to make Hope into an open jumper. These horses need to be alert, on the edge of their game at all times, and must jump substantial obstacles, which are very colorful, unusual and bright. The previous owner rode her with spurs and stick, intimidating her rather than educating her, and scaring this sensitive horse out of her mind on every schooling ride.

Hope wanted to please, but needed to understand the job. Without understanding, the mare became sullen and difficult. It had actually come to the point that when the previous owner entered the stall, the mare would run to the far corner, turn her hind end to the door, and threaten to kick. The mare, misunderstood, mismatched with rider and job description, was confused, scared and on the edge of psychotic breakdown.

The woman who sold her to me neglected to mention these problems. There was no mention of dangerous stall behavior, or poor attitude. Interestingly enough, however, Hope did not act in a bizarre way when she came to my farm. She was cautious and careful, keeping her distance from new people and new pasture mates, but never mean.

I didn't get the whole story until I had a visit from my veterinarian, about 45 days after I had purchased her. Dr. Cromer was at my farm to give the horses their spring vaccinations, a normal course of events for us. He walked into Hope's stall, took one look at her, and backed out quickly. Now Dr. Cromer is *no* slouch and he is not easily intimidated; he will work with the most disagreeable equines until he gets the job done. In this instance, however, he walked into Hope's stall and backed out quickly. He was not too happy seeing my new horse.

"What is *that horse* doing here!" he exclaimed. Turns out that he was also the veterinarian for Hope's previous owner and Hope had run him out of her stall on several occasions!

I looked at him in complete shock as he told me that this mare was not terribly trustworthy. In the past, he had felt that safety required this horse to be handled carefully and watched closely. Further, he regarded her as aggressive.

"Are you sure this is the same horse?" I asked, incredulous.

He peered into her stall again, checking. "Pretty mare, reddish gold body, white stockings, nice head, yep, it's the same horse. The whites of her eyes always used to show, like her eyes were going to pop out of her head. Maybe she looks a little quieter today, but I'm sure she is the same horse! Why is she here?"

This was the longest speech I'd ever heard from him. Dr. Cromer was sparing with words, kind and patient, and not quick to bad-mouth anyone, human or equine.

"Well," I told him, "I bought this horse a month and a half ago, and she was a little nervous at first, but she's getting quieter all the time. The more consistently I ride, the quieter she goes. I think that is a fair deal."

He thought a minute, and said, "Show me."

So, I walked into the stall, bridle in hand, and she greeted me at the door, with her polite end. No feet flying, no bared teeth, she just lowered her head and let me put the bridle on. Then I put the saddle on her back, tightened the girth, (okay, so I admit there was a little teeth-gnashing when I pulled the girth up; she *still* does that) . Then I mounted and rode off.

"Amazing," he said. "Watching you, I can't believe it is the same horse. Guess Hope found someone who understands her." And with that, he gave her the vaccinations.

Now, am I telling you that every horse can be rehabilitated with just the right situation? Absolutely not! However, Hope was a horse who had been misunderstood, treated roughly, and was merely protecting herself in the only way she could.

I feel at this point that I must mention there are some horses, just like some people, whose dark side is dominant. They don't play by the same rules as everyone else, nor do they value life. They are mean, caring little for themselves, and not at all for anyone else. Are they born that way, or do life experiences create the monster? I don't know, probably some of both. Regardless, there are *some horses, just like some people, who really do not wish to participate, relate or trust.* And I think it pays to be able to recognize these types, and avoid the heartache and danger.

Some horses really do not wish to participate, relate or trust.

It took me many years, lots of experience and a few bad accidents to discover that you can't save them all. How do you spot these? I can only offer some guidelines. Beyond that, you just have to decide for yourself. I would recommend asking a reputable trainer to help you if you are not skilled in this area.

I always look at the eyes of horses. I watch their posture, and try to read their body language. Unlike people, who often try to project what they want you to see, horses are generally honest. They show you their emotions, if you have the sense and patience to pay attention. If you approach quietly from the side, and the horse pins his ears and turns his back end to you, you probably should leave that one alone. If he spooks and shies at everything, seeing gremlins behind every bush, he's probably not the horse for an inexperienced rider. Still, such things do not make him a renegade.

Dangerous horses are in a category all their own, and you just have to develop a feel for recognizing them. There is something reckless in their attitudes. They are careless with themselves, not fearing for their own safety, and never careful about the safety of others. If you spend your lifetime with horses, you will see a few of these. Sour, incorrigible, spoiled. Always trying to be one step ahead of you, never willing to give a little, this type waits for your guard to be down. And then trouble happens. I have learned to be careful, because there are so many wonderful, talented and useful horses in the world. Look for them.

In Hope's case, when given patient handling and consistency, she became a very respectable citizen. She has foxhunted, been to horse shows and competed well, and recently has begun to

Horses need to know that someone is in charge

serve as a lesson horse. She still needs to be handled quietly. Loud, unexpected noises still scare her, but she has learned to stand her ground. She has developed real courage. *If you never know fear, then you can never be courageous. You have to know fear to conquer it.* And Hope, facing her fears, has shown courage when the situation calls for it. I wrote about the time she saved me. Would she save anyone, you might wonder, or was she just bonded to me? Or, perhaps, was the whole thing a fluke, an accident of time and place? You decide.

One of the jobs that I do on a daily basis is to choose a suitable horse for each lesson student to ride that day. I take that responsibility quite seriously, as the safety and success of that lesson depends on my selections. And I often teach 40 students per week, so every day I am faced with serious decision-making that can have far-reaching consequences. I try to match hyper folks up with placid horses, confident riders get horses that could use direction, timid riders will be matched with horses who are self-confident and quiet. Still, I must try to help each student grow in skill, all the while keeping them safe.

By way of example, I remember one lesson in particular. The evening was beautiful, the changing leaves colorful on the trees, the approaching sunset golden and serene. The horses were working well with the beginner to advanced-beginner riders, who knew how to walk, trot and canter, and could jump small obstacles. The four students in the ring took their turns, working on balance, control and technique. One boy, mounted on a thoroughbred-quarter horse cross, was not as attentive as I hoped he'd be. "Control your reins, Jacob" I admonished several times. "Horses need to know that someone is in charge. They need to know someone is driving."

Reins still flopping, I was just about to tell Jacob to pull up and stop, when he lost his balance, and completely lost his reins! The poor horse, now with no direction at all, began to pick up speed, looking about the ring with panic. "Pick up your reins, son. Just pick up your reins." But Jacob was beyond listening now, and he began to yell loudly, "WHOA! HELP ME! WHOA!

The horse was now sure the devil himself was in pursuit, and so he responded with the only thing he could control---speed. Faster and faster he went, with the rest of us aghast. Every riding instructor hates this scenario. Falling off a slow equine is uncomfortable enough. Falling off a panic-stricken one approaching warp speed is entirely another. "Jacob, look at me, come to me," I called. Sometimes eye contact with rider or horse can help. Jacob kept yelling. The horse kept running. The situation was deteriorating rapidly. Around and around the arena they went, gaining speed, increasingly out of control. Suddenly the boy's mother, in the same lesson and riding Hope, called his name. That familiar voice broke through his fear and he looked at her!

The horse went where the boy looked, straight toward his mother, and directly towards Hope. What would Hope do? Horses do not typically like confrontation, and Hope in particular was fearful of loud noises, including screaming children. I feared that she might wheel away, possibly unseating the mother. She also might kick at the intruder, not understanding why this other horse would invade her space.

We all live each day on the fine line between life and death, between good and evil, between that golden sunset and impending darkness. Today, we were caught for a brief moment in that time warp, the place where things could go one way or another. *And we were all afraid!*

Seeing the out-of-control horse approaching, Hope turned her back, presenting her ample hind-end, but she did not run. Lowering her head, she braced and once again, she **took the hit!** The boy's horse plowed directly into Hope at full speed, knocking the mother forward onto Hope's neck, but still the horse held her ground. The boy fell, nearly under her feet, but sustained bruises only. The scared, runaway horse stood still after the impact, no longer frightened because his rider was no longer yelling and silence was restored. There was no more screaming. And Hope, valiant Hope, had faced her greatest fears of noise and stress once again. She had conquered those fears and in the process she stopped the runaway horse and saved the young boy.

I'll never know who felt more grateful: the frightened boy, the terrified horse, the traumatized mother or me. *But we all agreed on one thing---we believed in Hope!*

Chapter 13

The "Darndest" Things

If the world was truly a rational place, men would ride side-saddle.

Rita Mae Brown

There used to be a guy on television named Art Linkletter, and he hosted a show appropriately called "Kids Say the Darndest Things". Even though I was a kid myself when this show was running, I loved it. The angle was that he would chat with a panel of kids, ask them questions, and then see what kind of answers he got. Well, most children are pretty forthright about what is on their minds, and they are not bothered by societal pressures of politically correct, polite or even what should or shouldn't be said. The filters created by years of living, of figuring out what is appropriate and what is not, those filters are just not there. Children are so fresh and natural and say what comes to the forefront of their consciousness.

Nearly every day I hear some of the "darndest" things that make teaching fresh and full of humor.

For example, I remember one sunny day, perfect temperature, and just the kind of day that makes riding horses so enjoyable. The dads and moms of the students were sitting ringside in the viewing area, watching their little darlings with interest and, dare we say it, amusement.

– Kali and Joey, campers

I was in the ring with four little boys, on four little ponies. This in itself was a recipe for hilarity. Picture it! Six and seven year old boys, not terribly interested in the finer points of equitation, are going around the riding ring, communicating their energy and eagerness to my ponies. Saintly though these ponies were, they could catch the energy vibe from these little boys from time to time. It was my job to nurture a love of horses and riding while keeping these little dudes alive.

I say, "Okay, boys, let's pick up a posting trot."

The boys hear "Race around the ring and try to get ahead of the kid in front of you" or "Can this pony go faster than the one next to it?"

Keeping order in such a group is always challenging. One particularly rowdy day, I resorted to bribery. "If you guys work with me, I will let you decide how we cool down the ponies at the end of lesson."

Sure enough, when lesson was over, Austin (one of my four riders) pipes up with "Can we ride bareback?"

Hmmmm…Keep in mind that these are four little boy beginners, who are still working on the basics of balance and control. While riding with saddles and stirrups posed no immediate safety issue, the lack of same could be another thing.

"Austin, you won't like bareback," I answered. "Why don't you ask for something else?"

"Come on, Miss Darlene, you *promised* we could pick!" This was the response from Austin. His voice easily carried across the riding ring. "Yeah, yeah," came a chorus of support from the other guys in the class. I was stuck. There was no way out, without breaking my word.

"Okay boys, off with the saddles!" What else could I do?

> ## Miss Darlene! I can feel this horse's vertebrane!

Once everyone had dismounted and removed their saddles (quite a process for six and seven year olds), I helped them remount. They began to walk around the ring riding bareback on their ponies. The ponies were good, the boys were happy, the parents were amused, and I had kept my word. I was counting my blessings, perhaps prematurely.

"How about if we trot," called Austin. "Yeah, yeah," answered his partners in crime.

"Guys, you won't like trotting bareback," I responded. "Let's just walk." I must repeat here that these were little beginners, whose balance and control were still in the developmental stages. And I must also mention that without balance and control, these little *boys* would not be able to protect their anatomy from hitting on the back and withers of their ponies if they trotted.

A chorus of support for trotting welled up from my students, so four boys began bouncing around on the ponies' backs. I really can't say who was more uncomfortable, the boys, the ponies or me. Once again, Austin spoke up. "Miss Darlene," he called in a very clear voice that carried across the ring, "Miss Darlene! I can feel this horse's *vertebrane!*"

"How about that, Austin," I responded. "Without the saddle you can feel the horses muscles and bones and the way that they move." Austin's Dad was smiling broadly at his son's choice of words. The other parents were smiling as well.

Pleased with the success of his first comments, Austin offered further clarification. "Miss Darlene," Austin called again, "Trotting bareback hurts my pee-pee!" This too was delivered in a very clear voice. Trying to keep a straight face, I chose to ignore this comment.

Not to be denied, Austin called in a louder, stronger, *clearer* voice, "Trotting hurts my pee-pee!"

From the sidelines, Austin's father calls, "That's enough, son. We get it."

Austin, thinking for a moment, came back with, "Well, I guess that does it for bareback!"

Yep, I guess it does…

◌৪৹

On another occasion, I was teaching a different student in the ring. He was doing well. He had mastered the walk, trot and canter, and seemed to be thoroughly enjoying himself. He was the son of a prominent physician in our area. Suddenly, he stopped his pony and walked over to me.

"What is it, Aaron?" I asked.

"I just really need to talk to you, Aaron replied. Coming closer, and leaning down toward me, he announced in an exaggerated stage whisper, "My Dad is a doctor!"

"That's great Aaron," I responded, wondering why he felt the need to share this detail now.

"Well, "he continued, in his exaggerated whisper, "I just want you to know that *he is not the malpractice kind of doctor!*"

Yes, indeed, kids do say the darndest things.

◌৪৹

Each summer we have camp here at the farm. Camp is where tired parents send their children for fun and games in the country while they try to shop, clean, work and regroup! Kids and equines do seem to be a great mix. It is our goal to foster a love of horses and improve skill levels and proficiency on horseback while keeping children alive and safe. The alive and safe part requires good camp counselors, good horses, and lots of good luck. Activities include riding horses (you might have guessed), hiking, water sports (otherwise known as horse washing), games on horseback, nature trails, etc. Some very memorable moments occur at camp, so I thought I'd share a few here.

One evening, after a strenuous day of riding, we decided to take our campers hiking. The trail was well marked, required no special equipment, and had nice rocks to rest on along the way. It was an uphill hike, and at the summit was a gorgeous outcropping of limestone where we could sit and look out over the valley. Each camper carried a sandwich and water bottle in their pack. This had all the makings of a gorgeous, carefree outing for campers and counselors alike.

Climbing to the summit, we all sat down on various rocks to eat our sandwiches and tell tales of our climb. Diana, my oldest daughter, had brought along her dog, Lily. Tying Lily's leash to a small tree growing out of the outcropping, she sat down to join us. Suddenly, the dog began barking and yelping, straining at the end of her leash! The cause became quickly apparent. There was a nest yellow-jackets at the base of the tree, and the bees were swarming the dog!

Lily had been the first to disturb their nest

Several of us ran forward to free the dog, but now the bees were very agitated, swarming primarily around Lily as she had been the first to disturb their nest.

"Everybody, start down the path!" I directed. "Let me go first! Then follow." It was my intention to pass by the nest first, so any still-angry bees would follow me, instead of swarming someone else. I don't like getting stung any more than the next person, but I am not sensitive to bees, and I wanted to protect my campers. My sister, Linda, mistaking my intention, yelled "No, I need to go first, because I'm allergic to bee stings!"

"No, Linda, don't do it," I'm yelling, but she didn't stop! Now our outing has become potentially lethal for both the dog, with multiple stings, and Linda, with severe bee sting allergies. Somehow, Linda got by the nest without incident, and all of us scrambled after her, and down the path for a quarter mile or so.

Lily the dog began to stumble, and then fell over on her side, breathing shallowly and rapidly. Oh no! Diana and I crouched down, examining her. "Quick, give me your water bottles," I called to the camp girls. They gladly offered their drinks, which I began to pour over the dog, trying to cool her off. Still she struggled with breathing and consciousness. "I need some Benadryl or an antihistamine." I was in a panic. Linda looked in her pack and produced an epi-pen, which she carries with her at all times. It can be the difference between life and death for those with severe allergies like hers. "I can't take your pen, Linda," "we just can't take the chance that you might need it!" I was very touched that she offered.

Lily was still struggling to breathe and the situation was looking grim. We were easily three miles hike from out vehicles, and beyond that, certainly another ten miles from a veterinarian. I didn't think the dog would make it that far. And Lily was a 90 pound boxer, so I wasn't sure we could cover much ground carrying her.

At that point, Megan, one of the older campers, came up to me. "Miss Darlene," she began, "I have a bottle of liquid Benadryl that I keep for when my allergies act up." Hope sprang up in my heart!

"Will you need this medicine to finish the hike?" I inquired?

"Nope. Haven't used it all day." was her response.

Taking the bottle of Benadryl, I poured about one third of it into the slack lips of the unconscious boxer. Then we waited for what seemed forever. I looked at Diana, and then at the faces of the campers, all gathered around us. Concern, fear, and disbelief registered on each set of eyes.

Thinking we were too late, I began to thank the girls for their calmness and supportive attitudes. "Sometimes, despite our best efforts, things just don't turn out the way we want them to." I wanted to comfort these young girls who had offered their water, their medication and their hopes.

"Look, Mom!" Diana croaked out between tears. "Look, she's waking up!"

And so she was! Lily looked rough, drunk almost, but she picked up her head and LOOKED at us. In a few more minutes, she staggered to her feet, and we again started down the path. It took a while, but we all made it back to the vehicles. The campers had a great story to share with their parents and friends, and I was again reminded that we all walk such a thin line between "everything is just fine" and "what in the world just happened".

CR80

Sometimes the events at camp are touching, like the day with the bees. Other days, things are just funny. On one such occasion, one of my counselors, Britni, was instructing a group of little campers, ages 6 to 8, about the parts of the horse. "This is the barrel (stomach area) of the horse, this is the poll (area between the ears), and this is the dock (where the tail is joined onto the horses body) . Britni, herself a product of numerous camps, pony club experiences, and lessons, used her best teacher voice. Knowing that children remember best when they practice, she had the campers repeat back to her the names of the equine body. The day went on, with each child grooming and riding the horse or pony assigned to them.

We all walk such a thin line

At the end of the day, the parents arrived to pick up their children. One of Britni's campers, a little blondy named Katie, eagerly grabbed her mother's hand and dragged her over to Britni, who was taking off the bridle and saddle from a camp pony.

"Mommy, I want to tell you what I learned from Miss Britni today," the child announced. As I watched this scene unfolding, I could see the pride in Britni's eyes, as she held the pony.

"Mommy, Miss Britni told me about the parts of the horse today. This is the "poll" (pointing to the top of the head), and this is called the "barrel" (indicating the largest, most round part of the horse's abdomen), and this is called the, um, what is it, um, oh yes, the "cock" (pointing at the root of the tail on top of the horse's body) ."

Britni inhaled sharply, then quickly corrected. "The base of the tale is actually called the" DOCK"! You almost had it right."

"Yes, Mommy, the" DOCK", that's what it is!" Little Katie repeated.

Britni, the mom, and I all smiled the nervous smile that occurs after such a *moment,* and we said our goodbyes for the day. Britni and I didn't dissolve into laughter until the last vehicle had pulled down the driveway.

Yep, kids do say the darndest things!

Chapter 14

Decisions, Decisions

There are only two emotions that belong in the saddle; one is a sense of humor and the other is patience.

John Lyons

How does one summarize a lifetime in 2000 words or less? Is a chapter enough to chronicle how the years have been spent? I don't know. I can only say it has been a roller coaster of a ride, and I'm not done yet.

Days flash by, almost unbelievably fast. Take yesterday, for example. When I got up, the temperature was 1 degree Fahrenheit, with a wind chill of -15 degrees. Now, this is not normal temperature for Virginia, which is in a temperate zone. I thank God for that fact, because I don't think I am cut out for 1 degree weather. But, when you are a "horse person", you do what you need to do. Even my troughs with water heaters were frozen on top. In the process of feeding in the morning, we discovered that one of our horses, Calvin, was having some sort of gastric distress. Colic! This is a word that every horse owner or caretaker knows and fears. Colic is essentially the word for "acute abdominal pain". We humans get that, babies are famous for it, and it generally resolves itself. We adults know that, in most cases, the pain will subside and whatever is troubling us will have been eliminated—one way or another—by the next day or so. Not so with horses!

Horses live in the moment, that is, their reality is what they are feeling or experiencing at any given moment of time. They have memory, some remember very well, but anything like acute, immediate pain is life-threatening to them. Perhaps because they are prey animals (animals likely to be eaten by others if they do not stay fit, healthy, and able to run away when threatened), or perhaps because they cannot see forward to a probable resolution of their pain, horses become frantic when painful. And so, while we can certainly say that Calvin was in no danger of being harmed by predators, his instincts were still strong.

A lipoma is a fatty tumor, non– malignant

He was desperate to find relief. And so, finding him in distress and during this extreme cold snap, I gave him a dose of Banamine, intravenously. Banamine, a non-steroidal anti-inflammatory drug, is known to help with some mild colic cases. It acts primarily on inflamed tissues, and thus is often helpful with colic. Then I called the veterinarian and Calvin's owners. Twenty minutes later, Calvin's pain was only marginally relieved, so I was most anxious for the vet to get to the farm. While waiting, I walked him slowly around the arena, talking to him and trying to keep him from dropping to the ground and rolling. Why is rolling a bad idea, you might wonder. That is because the horse carries around 120 feet of intestines with him at all times, so violent rolling can be quite problematic! If those intestines flop around and coil over on themselves, the horse can get a strangulation in his digestive system. When this happens, the outlook can be very grim.

While waiting for the vet, Calvin's owner's mom, Susan, arrived to help me. The vet arrived in about an hour, and after examination, she concurred with me the medications were not helping him. We decided to ship him to the Blue Ridge Clinic, about 1 hour away.

Calvin traveled well, and his owner, Ashley met us there. (She lives and works in Richmond. I think she must have rented a helicopter, because she got there very quickly!) Upon arrival, the doctors at the clinic began giving him a thorough examination, including an ultrasound. This medical study revealed a possible *lipoma*. A lipoma is a fatty tumor, non-malignant, that is suspended from the intestinal wall by a stalk, dangling the way a Christmas ornament hangs on a tree branch. Sounds rather non-threatening, but here's the rub: when you add this little gem into the stomach cavity already carrying 120 feet of intestines, things can get a little dicey! In Calvin's case, his lipoma and its stalk had gotten wrapped around 4 feet of his small intestine, causing that much of it to become necrotic or dead. Fecal matter could not pass through, and it would be just a matter of hours before he would die of peritonitis, getting poisoned by the toxins backing up in his system.

Surgery was the only answer. How can I describe the sorrow and anxiety in the eyes of Ashley and Susan? If you are a horse person and you are reading this, you know what I am talking about. If not, picture yourself talking to your best friend, and finding out that he or she must have invasive surgery *immediately*, or he or she will die. Imagine that you are looking at your friend and it is up to YOU to say if this friend will have this surgery, and YOU have to pay for it. Their life hangs in the balance...and YOU have to decide.

In my career with horses, I have been in this position several times. It is never easy. So, on this day, my job was to be a mentor to these two women as they made decisions for Calvin. We all prayed for Calvin's safety and for the knowledge and expertise of the surgeon.

We watched the surgery, all two and one-half hours of it, through the observation window. Dr. Trostle and his staff were amazing. They located the lipoma, removed it and the damaged 4 foot section of small intestine, reconnecting the healthy ends, and monitoring his vital signs and managing his anesthesia. I have seen such surgery several times. I still find it quite amazing! Prayers, hope and good medical care can be a winning formula!

So...Calvin is recovering well, one day post-surgery. His vitals are normal, he is hungry and his body is producing manure. All this is great. Still I am amazed at the fine line between the good and the bad, between survival and death, between absolute emotional devastation and the sweet relief of success.

How does this story about Calvin and the lipoma fit in with summarizing my life? Well, that's just it, you see. I take every day quite seriously…and still try to retain my sense of humor. I am quite aware the wrong decision can be a very serious thing when you are dealing with animals and people.

Every day I must choose the right horse for the right rider. If I pair up a feisty 1200 pound equine with a timid 130 pound human, bad things can happen. If I don't notice when an animal is not "right" (think Calvin), bad things can happen. If I make the wrong choices, I must look in the mirror and live with the consequences.

ᘓᘒᗭ

Another example of such choices would involve Thanks for the Memories. This mare, who would eventually be inducted into the

> ## *The wrong decision can be a very serious thing*

Southwest Virginia Hunter/Jumper Association Hall of Fame, came to us as a fractious three-year-old Trakehner mare, sired by Special Memories, a son of Abdullah, silver medalist in the 1984 Olympics. Well bred, we purchased this youngster as a resale prospect. In short order, however, both Brooke (my youngest daughter) and I fell in love with her. Love/hate might be more like it. At three, "Marcy" was incorrigible! Difficult to ride, prone to rear straight up like a rocket, many others (including some very good trainer friends) felt that she was too risky for my 15 year old daughter to ride. Brooke, however, was totally on board with trying to get this mare to the show ring. The horse had jumping talent, and even more, she had "heart", that intangible something that horses (and people) either have or they don't.

At first Marcy, the barn name for Thanks for the Memories. would enter the show ring dancing around on her two hind feet. This is not typically regarded as a good thing! I could see disapproval on the faces of some of the spectators as they watched me bring Marcy to the ring, and then let her go with my child on board. I knew the risks. I had thought long and hard about whether the risk was too great. Was I risking Brooke's safety? Possibly...ok, yes. But we saw something bold, beautiful and worthy of trust when we looked at the bay mare.

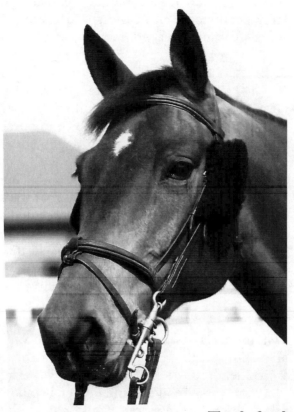

– Thanks for the Memories

Getting Marcy to the first fence was difficult, but once she focused on the jump, she became all business. She loved jumping, and she looked forward to each new jumping challenge. When she was five, Brooke and I travelled down to Gulfport, Mississippi, to do the show series there. Marcy was a superstar! She and Brooke became a formidable force in the junior jumper classes. The jumps were sizable, but the heart and "try" of this team was even bigger.

For the next eight years, Brooke and Thanks for the Memories (Marcy) graduated from junior classes to open classes, eventually competing at Grand Prix level. A feed company utilized their images on their performance feed bags. We travelled extensively, from Virginia to Washington, D. C., doing the Washington International Horse Show. We traveled south to Gulfport and Ocala. We showed the mare in Roanoke, Lexington (Virginia and Kentucky), Maryland, New Jersey, you get the idea. Always giving her best, Marcy competed well in the speed class at Upperville, finishing third against such great competitors as Margie Engle and Joe Fargis.

> *I have tried to produce horse people, not just riders.*

So, what does this have to do with my life? Clearly, making the choice to follow a horse career, making the choice to purchase such a horse, making the choice to allow my daughter to ride at this level and to ride a horse with a few "quirks", all of this has been a part of the adventure.

We had disagreements along the way. Once, a trainer we were working with at the time felt that adding a more severe bit (the metal device the horse wears in their mouth) and a yank and pull method to riding would control the always-aggressive Marcy and help us win more classes. He also felt that fast was better than accurate. For a short while, this pied piper kind of appealed to Brooke. I forgive her. She was very young and very eager to learn this difficult level of work. Being around longer, I could see that too much bit and crash-and-burn riding would quickly burn out my horse, and possibly injure her and my kid.

Again, hard choices. At the risk of losing favor with my child, and at the risk of being viewed as an interfering trainer, mother and horse owner, I did the only thing I could do. I took my horse and my daughter home. I began to search for another trainer, one who would have the best interests of my horse and my daughter foremost in his/her mind. We needed a trainer who understood their strengths and their limitations, and who was willing to work to improve both horse and rider. I had gotten her this far. I had instilled in Brooke a love of horses, a great work ethic, and I had given her a good start with her riding. She was a very competent rider. But I had never worked at Grand Prix level. I just never had that kind of horse or support along the way. Now we needed a trainer to take her to the next level, teach her well and weigh the risks for her and her horse. We found one! (Thank you, Paul!) He became a great mentor for her and her horse, fine tuning the skills she came with, teaching her accuracy and timing, giving her the skills she now uses as a professional rider out on her own. We owe a lot to this man and his wife. Both recognized Brooke's talent and drive, and her willingness to learn.

– Brooke riding in Grand Prix in Tryon, 2014

I sometimes wonder what my greatest life contributions have been. I know that during my 30 years in the horse industry, I have started numerous riders. Some went on to be horse professionals, some have continued to ride as amateurs, still others are now bringing me their children to teach. One family is now in their third generation with me, as I taught the mother, her daughter, and now her daughter's daughter. (Truthfully, this makes me feel a little old, but you must realize I was just a baby when I began teaching you, Elizabeth!)

I have tried to produce horse people, not just riders. It's not enough to just get on a horse and bop around. I want those who learn from me to regard the horse as a living, breathing creature that depends on us humans for its care and comfort. Equines overcome their instincts as a prey animal, and offer us their service and their willingness to do our bidding. They trade these things for our companionship, our concern and our kindness. We must never take these things for granted.

Hopefully those who have learned from me know there are no short cuts to success. You have to put in the time and effort. Hopefully they have learned the horse must come first, as they cannot fend for themselves in our domesticated environment. No horse in his/her right mind would volunteer to jump over a 1. 40 meter course of fences, except that they have been well-trained by their human and trust that person to help them. No horse with good sense would voluntarily let beginner riders yank on the reins and pull on their mouth, or flop around in the saddle (on their backs) like a sack of potatoes. Such a horse has learned the humans have to learn to ride well, and so the horse puts up with this unintentional abuse because we ask them too.

I hope that those whom I have taught have learned to be attentive to detail. Are the straps too tight on this blanket? Are the horse's shoes loose? Does this one look a little lame in the right front?

Does my saddle fit well, or is it pinching my horse's withers? Is the horse getting enough feed, or too much? Does this horse have enough training to do *this* job? Is it *fair* to ask the horse to do this job?

I celebrate the love of the horse every day. As I have said before, I am firmly convinced the development of humans and the development of equines have been intertwined since ancient times. Some humans recognize and act on this DNA directive, while it is recessive in others. If you've got it, you've got it. It's that simple. And if indeed you've got it, by golly, it should be nurtured.

Yep, that's what I do...

Chapter 15

All in a Day's Work

Life ain't certain…ride your best horse first.

Anonymous

Working with animals ten times human size can be challenging, amusing, terrifying and rewarding, sometimes all at the same time. Certainly I can say grace over many experiences that would fit in this category.

I distinctly remember one day at the Rockingham County Fairgrounds. Parked in the big grassy field, I was preparing one of my show horses for his classes in the show. Deciding that he needed some water, I walked over to the fence line and turned on the pump. Waiting for my bucket to fill, I heard some yelling from the overflow parking area. Looking in that direction, I saw a four horse trailer parked on the other side of the fence.

"Help me, HELP me," came the voice from within that trailer. Well, horse emergencies happen quickly, and quick intervention can be the difference between a scary situation and a tragic one. So I took off running toward the trailer and the voice.

Inside, a fellow horse professional, Jo, stood looking at her horse, who had jumped the front stall partition and was dangling, front feet on one side and hind feet on the other. He looked like an equine see-saw, rocking back and forth on the chest bar in front of him. Clearly in distress, the horse was mashing his own diaphragm on the stall front, made of a stout metal bar. Thrashing around, the horse would touch first his hind feet on the floor of the trailer and then he would attempt to launch himself forward. Of course, this action only served to make him more winded, because he was resting squarely on the metal bar with his chest and belly. He couldn't get himself free! Loosening the trailer ties that kept his head up, I tried to release the closure pin on the metal bar, hoping to allow him to fall to the floor, thus freeing himself. But the horse was easily 1100 pounds, and I couldn't budge him. Even getting Jo to help me, the two of us could not move the bar enough to unlatch it. By now it was clear...we needed help.

I ran down the trailer ramp, with Jo yelling at me. "Going for help!" I yelled back, as I headed toward the main parking area.

Sprinting across the field I too began to yell.

"I NEED A MAN! I NEED A MAN!" I shouted as loudly as I could. It was only quite a bit later that I realized my choice of words left a lot open to interpretation.

Looking up, several guys began to run towards me! As I reversed direction, I waved at them and indicated that they should follow me. Racing around the corner of the fence, I approached the horse trailer, and directed "my" men to come inside. Once in, the reason for my yelling became abundantly clear. One of the guys got a tire iron and wedged it under the latch where the horse hung, now very still and limp. I said a silent prayer that we weren't too late.

With two guys pushing on the tire iron and another pushing on the bar, the latch finally gave way, and we all jumped back as the horse crashed to the ground. He lay still as death, and hardly seemed to be breathing. We all looked at each other as Jo began to sob.

Then, after what seemed an eternity, the horse heaved a great breath of air into his lungs and began to scramble to him feet! Success! Within a few minutes, we were treating his various scrapes and cuts, but there was no permanent damage done. Jo slowly walked him off the trailer, allowing him to rest and graze in the field.

"Wow, guys," I began. "Don't know what we would have done without you. Thank you so much!"

All three were very brave, having put themselves in danger to rescue this horse. Horse people are generally like that, though. We usually rise to the occasion and help each other. Kind of like an unwritten code. Still, I repeated thanks on behalf of Jo and myself.

As our three rescuers were leaving, one of them stopped to quip, "My pleasure, ma'am!" Then he added "You know, this wasn't quite what I expected when I heard a lady yell about needing a man!"

"HA!"

⚬⚬

Back in the early 1980's, it was not uncommon to attend all-breed shows. That means that multiple disciplines and styles of riding would be represented. The hunters, jumpers, western pleasure, racking horses, and Tennessee Walkers would all share the same

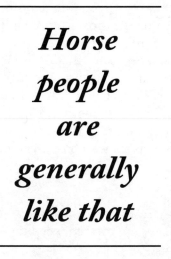

Horse people are generally like that

venue, showing at different times. This memorable day was a hot one, one of those cookers that makes you wonder why you chose horses over ice hockey, or something. Anyway, my truck and trailer just happened to be parked next to a lady who was obviously showing a walking horse. For those not familiar, walking horses show on the flat, with gaits remarkably different than the hunter horses I was used to.

In the hunter world, show clothes consist of tan breeches, a conservative shirt, topped off with a wool coat in an equally conservative grey, brown, or navy. The horse was to be impeccably clean and equally traditionally turned out.

Walking horse costuming was decidedly different. This lady was going to be well dressed in a green sequined jacket and black pants. Her horse was absolutely clean, with a spotless white mane and tail which nearly sparkled when it moved. It is common for the walking horse folks to add a false tail, which contributed to a long flowing appearance. The woman had matching platinum blond hair, teased and sprayed. Her hair exactly matched the color of horse's tail. I will never know if that was by accident or design! Either way, this pair was well-groomed by the standards of their discipline.

With her class coming up, the woman was putting the final touches on her horse, and then she tacked him up. Saddle and bridle in place, she left the horse for a moment to run into her trailer for her sequined jacket. Chartreuse green, it shimmered in the sunlight as she emerged from her dressing room. Studying the entire picture, she paused for a moment, and then decided to give that flowing tail one more swipe of the brush.

As if on cue, or perhaps giving evidence to some show nervousness, the horse lifted his tail, and without further ado, SPRAYED his rider, sequins and all, with the loudest, nastiest, and most liquid manure you could ever imagine!

In what one could call a pregnant moment, the woman's face registered disbelief, shock and then, well, then I couldn't control myself any longer. From deep inside me came the most irrepressible, unbelievable and distinctly irreverent gale of laughter.

"Oh no. I'm sorry. Oh no." I tried to choke back my inappropriate outburst of laughter, but I really had no control. This was about the funniest thing I had ever seen. If I had access to a video then, I am sure we would have won America's Funniest, or something.

Totally out of control, we both turned and ran. The lady went to her dressing room, and I RAN to mine, both trying to clean up a messy situation!

ಶಿಶಿ

I feel I would be remiss if I didn't share some of the "Rules" or "Truisms" of the horse profession. Here are my top ten, keeping in mind that it would be easy to list the top 50!

Most horse emergencies happen late at night, in the coldest weather. Count on it, plan for it and be prepared.

90 percent of horse customers and clients are wonderful and a pleasure to have around. The other 10 percent will give you grey hair, indigestion and headaches. Count on it, plan for it and be prepared.

Riding comes with a certain amount of hazardous duty…either riding or handling horses. They are big, they are prone to run first and ask questions later, and sometimes they react hysterically (by human standards) . If you love them, and enjoy working with them, accept this and learn to think like a horse. Your safety depends on it.

Living with horses requires early mornings and late nights. The days are long. If you don't like the sound of those hours, don't become a horse professional.

Learn to think like a horse. Your safety depends on it.

If you don't know something, or have a question with no answer, find someone who genuinely knows more than you do. The source of answers is usually not the loudest voice of advice, and doesn't _necessarily_ have the most accolades or letters behind their name (Dr., PHD., etc.), although such authorities may very well contribute to your education. Listen to those who have been there and done that, study their suggestions, add this to your own store of knowledge, and above all, _do no harm._

Never stop learning. You will never know it all. No matter how well you do what you do, there will always be more to learn. This job is a lifetime commitment to learning.

Each horse is an individual, and even though it carries characteristics specific to its species, it is still an individual. That fact is both beautiful and puzzling. Enjoy it. No horse comes with an owner's manual. You must make educated guesses and learn from that individual every day.

Try to achieve balance between your personal life and your "horse life". This is not easy to do because most horse folks find the lines blurred between personal and professional enjoyment of horses. Try to take a vacation that lets you relax and be "off duty" once in a while. Find a "second in command" that you trust. Leave them in charge occasionally. They need the practice and you need the down time. (I struggle with this.)

Brush up on your people skills. The customer is there to _enjoy_ his/her horse or lesson, not to listen to your problems. We are in the "entertainment" industry. We are not the only show in town. Be sure that coming to your barn is safe, fun, inviting and meets the customer's needs.

Always have a Plan B. What is Plan B? It is the organized answer to the failure of Plan A.

I'm cutting myself off there. You are smart. You love horses. That's a great start. Good luck. As Jerry Shulman (horse-lover/ author) has said, "*His hooves pound the beat, your heart sings the song.*"

Oh, yeah, that's what I'm talking about.

— Savannah, Darlene and Willow at Lexington

Chapter 16

The Horse Life

"Whatever your purpose in riding, be sure that it includes the elements of fun and appreciation of your horse. Then you will be well on your way to becoming a true horseman."

Sheila Hundt

What is it like, living the "horse life"? Would I choose it all over again, given the option? What are the advantages, the disadvantages? Would I recommend this lifestyle to another?

Hmmm. These are tough questions, with no easy answers. Maybe I should tackle them one by one.

"Living the horse life" is different for different people. It can be owning one or two horses, and dedicating your discretionary time to riding. Horse involvement can be as simple as taking lessons on horses belonging to someone else. Or perhaps you are a professional rider, training and competing your own or client-owned horses. Maybe you run a horse-boarding facility or give riding lessons.

The horse life for me means getting up in the morning thinking about horses, and going to sleep at night doing the same thing. My passion, my work and my recreation have all been intertwined. I manage a boarding facility, teach riding lessons, attend many horse shows per year, host horse shows at my farm each year, and help students find suitable horses to ride and show, as needed.

In my role as barn owner and manager, I am responsible for the feeding and care of each horse on my property. Just like us humans, no two horses are alike, and so must have a feed and training plan tailored to their individual needs. That's my job. I must arrange for stalls to be cleaned, rings to be dragged (to keep the footing in good shape for the horses' feet), jumps to be painted, fences to be maintained, water troughs to be washed and bleached, farrier visits scheduled, veterinarian visits coordinated, and, well, you get it. This is a FULL TIME JOB. No, more than that, more than a full time job. If I counted every moment spent, either performing these functions, or arranging for them to be done, I guess I'd be making about $3. 00 per hour! *When you run a barn, you charge by the job, not by the minute or hour.*

If you are a person who wants to start work at 9 a. m. and finish by 5 p. m., then you don't want to be a professional stable owner.

Then, we have the lesson program. Daily, I hold my students' safety, *their very lives,* in my hands! It is an awesome and daunting responsibility. When I match a student up with a school horse, I am trying to provide them with an equine who is challenging enough to help them learn and further their training, but the horse

Fear cancels out learning

must also be safe enough to let them live! Equines are roughly 10 times the size of their riders, and it is only through their good training, their generous natures, and the bond that can be forged between equine and rider, it is only through these developments that students are able to learn to ride. The rider must not be afraid, because fear cancels out learning. But the rider cannot be smug, either, as overconfidence leads to carelessness and accidents.

I love teaching. It is perfect for me, as I love horses and people…sometimes in that order. I have ridden most of my life, but this is not enough. You must also know how to communicate the "how to" part, to teach in a variety of ways, because people learn in a variety of ways.

So, it is my job to eliminate as much fear as possible by providing suitable school horses for students to ride on and learn. Fear is the "mind killer". Students cannot learn if they fear for their lives, whether that fear is rational or not. I seek to share my love of equines with my students, teaching them from the ground up. I believe in teaching my students to be horsemen and horsewomen, not merely riders.

What is the difference between rider and horseperson? A rider climbs aboard a horse, spends time in lesson or show, then gets off and returns the horse to its handlers, to be cared for and put away. What a shame to approach riding in this way! A horseperson learns about the horse as a species, learns what it takes to keep equines happy and healthy, learns about veterinary care, shoeing, learns how the horse thinks, about the "why" behind its behavior. And then a horseperson takes the time to know what is required to become a partner with a specific, individual horse.

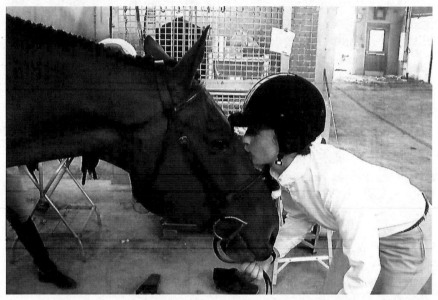

– Jordan kissing Joop

It is my sincere hope the students who have ridden with me have become "horsepersons", men and women who value the horse for what it is, friend, companion, and trusted partner.

When thinking of whether or not I would choose this profession again, I have to say "yes". Sure, I would not miss the long hours, sure I would love to get better pay, and I would definitely appreciate forty hour weeks rather than fourteen hour days (or longer) .

I wish I hadn't been so stressed by injured horses, sick foals, sassy students, or aggravating parents. Luckily, the eager students and the cooperative, supportive parents outnumber the difficult ones! But the bottom line is this: if I have shared my love of horses and all things equine with the majority of my students, and if I have improved the quality of life for the horses and ponies in my care, and if my students and my own children have come to cherish and appreciate horses as much as I do, then my career choice was the right one.

Emerson once wrote: *"We find delight in the beauty and happiness of children that makes the heart too big for the body."* I certainly agree. Replace "children" in this quote with "students ", and it is a perfect quote for me.

What follows are some of the cards and notes that I have received from my students over the years. This is a sampling that will perhaps help the reader to understand what this life, this "horse life", has meant to me.

This is a card that I received from a student who went on to become a veterinarian.

"Dear Darlene,
I cannot tell you how lucky I feel that Romeo and I ended up at your farm. After so many years of struggle and dismissal, we finally found a translator who was able to put us in a happy partnership of clear communication. You were the model of patience and novelty in problem solving. It's thrilling to be able to go around the ring in quiet gaits—in both directions! O. k., so maybe not thrilling to most, but after 10 years it is pretty darn spectacular to me. I hope an inkling of my appreciation is felt, for when all is well with a girl and her horse...all is well.
Thank you,
Sha"

꧁꧂

Another student wrote:

"Dear Darlene,
Thank you so much for helping me to become the rider I am today. I have many goals set before me and I know, with your help, I will be able to accomplish many of them. Thanks again for helping some of my dreams come true.
Love, Amanda"

꧁꧂

This is an excerpt from an interview I did with Jean, a James

Madison University student. She was researching careers. This is what she had to say:

"…She opened my eyes to all the downsides of owning your own horse farm AND all the rewards. I understand that my vacations won't be entirely spent at the beach, because I will be busy running a farm and trying to teach someone how to communicate with a horse. Leisure time is NOT one of the perks of the job. It's a life time of work to attain your own horse farm, and it's a life time to maintain. It's a stack of never ending paperwork and a life time supply of manure. It consists of days that start early and end late at night. One day, I hope to see if it's a life style that will suit me.

Jean M."

⊂⊃

Darlene, you are the best riding teacher ever. When you had the Ride For A Cure this year, your leg hurt but you didn't give up.

A memory that I'll never forget is my first ride. The second I got on Blaze, I knew that horses were a big part of my life. You helped me discover that, so thank you.

I admire the understanding you have for horses. You know when and what horses need. You don't make me do anything I don't want to do, but you push me to try new things.

Love,
Jules

– From a Student

And last, I include a note from Sue, a long- time friend. Our connection was made through horses. She helped me proofread some of the chapters included in this book. She offered this, and I include it in her words:

"Darlene does have a unique connection with horses. She is not the only one in the world who has this gift, but I think it is a rare gift. She really does have an unusual "heart" for horses and I saw this from what I have personally observed.

Many times I have seen her stop and look intently into the eyes of a horse and appear to be just listening. Then she will step back, think for a moment, and say something to a rider like, 'Do me a favor, would you? Get off a minute and change that saddle pad.' And with that small but significant adjustment, the horse becomes more comfortable and the problem is solved.

Even more dramatic is seeing her wake from total sleep, and head to the barn because one of the horses was calling to her, not out loud, mind you, but calling her all the same. And it would turn out that a horse needed something. Either she would discover a horse with colic, or a horse that had gotten 'cast' in the stall, rolling up against a wall and unable to free itself.

I have seen her, dead tired, get her boots on and head to the stable late at night, in the cold or any element, just to check on all of her charges. She would insist that all good horse people would do the same. But I insist that this connection is her 'gift,' and I give a resounding 'yes' to the title of this book.

It is about Darlene's horses and Darlene's heart. What good fortune for both."

There have been other occasions, other days and other messages, but such messages have made it all worth it. I have loved the horses, the people, and the lifestyle, be it ever so inconvenient, glorious or humbling.

The Tale of "Tex" and Rusty

One day I got a call, I think it was the Fall
    "Tex," said the stranger, "is my name."
"All my life I have been ridin', but my ridin's been a-sliding,
    And now I'm a little off my game."

"I am a little rusty, my boots a little dusty.
    A tune-up ride would really set me straight.
Please can't you teach me, oh yes, he did beseech me?
    I'll pay quite well if you will take the bait."

Oh no, I thought sadly, I think this might go badly.
    Tex sounds very dude-like to be sure.
But being rather broke, my pride I guess I'll choke.
    A tune-up ride for Tex might be the cure.
I saddled up ol' Rusty, I knew that he'd be trusty.
    He'd tolerate a dude without a doubt.
Rusty, sure and steady, had patience always ready,
    Bad riding wouldn't make ol' Rusty pout.

Tex showed up right on time, his new boots they did shine.
    His belt buckle could double as a plate.
His spurs jingled loudly, and Rusty's eyes went cloudy…
    He wondered what he'd done to draw this fate.
"To start this tune-up ride, just put those spurs aside."
    I said this to Tex, for safety's sake.
If you stick those big spurs in him, and then he goes to spinnin'
    Well, I think that spurs could be a big mistake.

So I checked the girth, dropped the spurs to earth,
    "Mount-up, it's time to ride" I told this dude.
The thing that happened next had us all a little vexed.
    Me and Rusty, well, we both thought that it was crude.
Tex picked up the reins, he did NOT consult his brains,
    Put his RIGHT foot in the stirrup nice and high.
In the stirrup he did stick it, and the left foot he did kick it
    Over Rusty's head and down the other side.

Now you know that I'm not joking, in fact I'm almost croaking,
    Never have seen this happen. What a sight!
Tex was sitting in the saddle, both legs were quite a-straddle
    But he was facing Rusty's tail—and that ain't right.

The moral of this story, whether for your gain or glory,
    Never brag or put your foot into your mouth.
Humble you should be, no tune-up ride you see
    Could help if you are riding facing south.

– Rusty

Epilogue The Pony Song

My daughter, Diana, handed me a piece of paper on the day of her wedding, just before she and her new husband, Wes, drove off to start their lives as a new family. On this piece of paper was written the lyrics of a song I used to sing to both of my children when they were little. They called it the "pony" song.

> Yesterday a child came out to wonder
> Caught a dragonfly inside a jar
> Fearful when the sky was full of thunder
> And tearful at the falling of a star
>
> And the seasons they go 'round and 'round
> And the painted ponies go up and down
> We're captive on the carousel of time

We can't return, we can only look
Behind from where we came
And go 'round and 'round and 'round
In the circle game

Then the child moved ten times 'round the seasons
Skated over ten clear frozen streams
Words like "when you're older" must appease her
And promises of "someday" make her dreams

And the seasons they go 'round and 'round
And the painted ponies go up and down
We're captive on the carousel of time
We can't return, we can only look
Behind from where we came
And go 'round and 'round and 'round
In the circle game

Sixteen springs and sixteen summers gone now
Cartwheels turn to car wheels through the town
And they tell her, "take your time, it won't be long now
"Till you drag your feet to slow the circles down"

And the seasons they go 'round and 'round
And the painted ponies go up and down
We're captive on the carousel of time
We can't return, we can only look
Behind from where we came
And go 'round and 'round and 'round
In the circle game

So the years spin by and now the child is twenty
Though her dreams have lost some grandeur coming true
There'll be new dreams, maybe better dreams and plenty
Before the last revolving circle is through

And the seasons they go 'round and 'round
And the painted ponies go up and down
Were captive on the carousel of time

We can't return, we can only look
Behind from where we came
And go 'round and 'round and 'round
In the circle game
And go 'round and 'round and 'round
In the circle game.

Joni Mitchell, The Circle Game

May you always enjoy your "ponies" and your "circles". D

Horses I have known and loved... in alphabetical order...

All That Jaz	Candy	Doc
Allie	Carrie	
Arabelle	Cash	Emma
	Cat Can Do	Faith
Baby	Cedar	Falcon
Bailey	Chance	Flicka
Bambi	Chandler	Fred
Bamboo	Charlie	Frosty
Bandit	Chase the Moon	
Bar Maid	Cherish	Garrett
Beastie	Cherub	Gemmie
Bellazadoc	Chip	George of the Jungle
Ben	Chuck	Gibbs
Bentley	CJ	Gilly
Beowolf	Classified	Ginger
Black Onyx	Cocoa	Good as Gold
Blaze	Cocoa	Gunner
Blue Moon	Coffee	
Bo Irvin	Copper	Handsome Ransom
Bones	Copy Cat	Hank
Bonnie View	CousCous	Harley
Boomer	Cover Girl	Hendrix
Brandy	Custom Made	Hershey
Bucky	Daisy Mae	Hocus Pocus
Buggy	Dallas	Holly
Buster Jones	Darla	Hope
Call Me Mister	Dasher	Huck
Calvin	Dilly	
Camille	DJ	I B Mikey

I Do   Nicholas   Stormy
Immigrant   Sunday
Isabella   Oliver   Sunshine

Jasper   Padre   Tally Ho
Jelly Bean   Panther   Teacher's Pet
Jemimah   Peachy   Teddy
Jilly   Penny   Tex
Joop   Peter   Thanks for the
Julie   Pip   Memories
Juliet   Prince William   Tickle Me
                        Purdy   Tilly
KC   Time Will Tell
Khan   Raja   Timmy
                        Renato   Tino
Leda   Rheilly   Toi's Ploy
Levi   Rhythm and Blues   Tommy
Lilly   Right Way   Treasure
Limited Square   Ring the Bell   Trey
Lois   Robin Hood   Trick or Treat
Louie   Rockin' Robin   Trust Fund
                        Romeo   Tucker I
Made in the Shade   Rudi   Tucker II
Magic Sprinkles   Twilight
Magic Sprinkles   Safari
Mago   Sami   Uptown Girl
Majik   Sandy
Major   Sargent Pepper   Where's Waldo
Malibu Barbie   Secret   Whiskey
Mandy   Shell   Whisper
Mark   Short Story   Wildfire
Maverick   Silver Slippers   Windsor Castle
Max a Million   Silver Tab   Woodwind
Merlin   Snooki   Woody
Milo   Snoopy
Misty D   Southbound   Yogi
Misty Morning   Squire
Molly   Stella   Zach
Moses   Sterling Silver   Zeba
Muffin   Stewball

"Apologies to any horses left out, but still appreciated."